Mixing Up Some Happiness

A Collection of Family Favorite Recipes
Across the Miles and the Years

Compiled by
Virginia K. White

Virginia K. White

The Year: 2020
Why This Book Was Important To Write

How will most people remember the year 2020? It has been a challenging one for most of us. From illness to quarantine to political arguments to protests to record setting and life-threating wildfires to relentless hurricanes and tropical storms, our world as we have known it seemed to be shredding itself apart. Personally, I needed something life-affirming, positive, and uplifting! In years past, I remembered that when days were dreary, I often baked. During our current troubling situation, I read over and over again that people were doing more cooking while quarantined. They seemed to be seeking solace by creating some family favorites. So, one day as I was mixing up what has now been called Grandma Cookies, I thought, "I think we all need to mix up some happiness!" Clearly that seemed to be what many people were doing to bring some happiness into their lives by cooking up some favorites. Perhaps it was time to share.

During this time of struggle, I was also researching my great grandmother's pioneer journey through Kansas and Nebraska. The thing that always brought her family together was food and the memories that went with it. Family favorite foods when they could find them and the memories that went with the food and preparation were constantly highlighted. So, I thought it might be worth seeing what recipes and memories other people had from years past. What were some favorite foods, the reason they were favorites, and what made the prepared dishes special? It seemed like sharing was something people wanted to do.

So I thought, "What if I put those favorites into a cookbook?" I threw that idea out to a few friends and received immediate favorable feedback. People said things like "What a great idea," and "I have some of my mother's recipes," and "I remember cooking with my grandmother and the recipe was only in her head, but it always came out scrumptious." I continued to reach out through email, Facebook, and again in person to see if people would submit favorite recipes with an explanation as to why the recipe was a favorite. My email, Facebook, and texts exploded with enthusiasm, recipes, and memories. People passed the word on to friends and more recipes and memories flooded in. It appeared as if everyone wanted to reach back to happier times and I was delighted to give them a reason to do that. Desserts clearly turned out to be the most popular submission. It was a mass gravitation toward sweet memories.

Along with the memory search for favorite recipes came the question of where these recipes were housed. Those of us who are seniors remember that recipes were not always written down. They were passed down through memory and included directions such as "a pinch of this," or "a handful of that," or "butter the size of a walnut." Because hand sizes varied, adjustments had to be made. Most recipes began as cultural favorites and eventually those cultural favorites varied in ingredients and amounts, depending on availability and desire, yet always produced a delicious product for family and friends.

My father was Czech and my great grandmother's pioneer journey sent me to not only physical research areas she talked about, but to textual research areas. One of the most fun areas of research was discovering Czech favorite recipes. Eventually some Czechs decided to write down recipes, but I discovered numerous recipes for favorites such as the Kolache. It seemed that each family varied the recipes much as we do today in order to suit our preferences and diet. I don't think my Grandmother Spinar ever wrote down a recipe or even had a recipe book or box. All preparation was housed in her head and everything she made was amazing! I remember asking her once how she made Kolaches and she showed me as she made it. There was no "a cup of this," or "1/2 teaspoon of that." She just knew and the finished product was always delicious.

Eventually someone thought it would be a good idea to collect recipes and put them into a book or write them on a card that would be housed in a box. Community cookbooks developed as well as school, and family cookbooks. Most early cookbooks did not have pictures, but just having the ingredients written down was everything needed to create the desired dish.

Companies often advertised in some of the cookbooks as well as created their own cookbooks. My father worked for Metropolitan Life Insurance Company for years and while cleaning out his house, I discovered several of these small cookbooks. KFOR, a Lincoln, Nebraska, radio station, still publishes small cookbooks and they continue to be popular today.

Favorite recipes were given to brides-to-be along with a recipe box so the bride would have ideas for cooking for her new husband and future children.

While researching for this book, I went through my mother's recipe books and her recipe box. Not only did I find recipes I'd given her, but some very old ones that said things like "Make a nice little cake and add carrots" to make a carrot cake. Or, "Bake in a moderate oven," but no clue as to how long or the exact temperature.

Today you can search the internet and find any number of recipes. People write blogs about food preparation and there are numerous cooking shows giving viewers not only recipes but a "how to step by step" for each recipe. Food magazines abound and one can search to find everything from seasonal recipes to recipes for special diet needs.

Throughout this book you will find simple and quick recipes to more elaborate ones. The thread they all have in common is that each recipe is a favorite and the love of family and friends is the reason those dishes are prepared again and again.

I also decided it would be fun to show a few pictures of some of those old recipe cards and boxes as well as the covers of a few community, school, church, and family recipe treasures. On the following pages you will find illustrations from my research.

Finally, I am a retired English teacher and I as I began working on this, I recalled numerous authors who included thoughts about food in their books. Or, if not in their novel, play, or short story, in their life style and time period. Hence, I decided to select a few of my favorite quotations and authors to share with you throughout the book.

I would like to thank everyone who enthusiastically embraced this project and submitted family favorite recipes. A special thanks to Staci Day, a former student and extraordinary art teacher, who agreed to do the layout design of this book.

It is my hope that you, as readers, not only enjoy reading the recipes and the stories that accompany them, but you find the quotations and pictures of interest as well.

Orange Ice box Cookies
1 cup shortening ¾ cup white sugar
¾ cup brown sugar
2 eggs 3½ cups flour 1 tsp. soda
grated rind of 1 orange

Put in refrigerator over nite

Mrs Heine

Chocolate Cake (very good)
½ c shortening 1½ cups sugar, 1 tsp. vanilla
3 whole eggs 2¼ squares melted chocolate
1½ c flour 1 tsp B. powder 1 tsp soda
pinch of salt 1 c sour cream. Cream shortening
add sugar & vanilla then chocolate
add beaten eggs Continue beating Add
dry ingredients with the cream alternately
Bake in moderate oven

Sample Old Recipe Cards

English Apple Pie
Peel & slice enough apples to fill baking
dish in which you put ½ c sugar
then mix ½ c butter ¾ c flour ¾ c B. sugar
Put lid on when baking so B. sugar
on top won't get hard

Marshmallow Dessert.
1 cup milk
1 lb. marshmallows
Put in double boiler and melt
Let stand till cold
Add 1 pt whipping cream whipped
1 cup shredded pineapple

Roll 8-10 graham crackers and
sprinkle bottom of dish. Pour in above
mixture sprinkle more crumbs on top
Chill 24 hrs

Recipe box Connie Hirz received at her bridal shower

Carrot Cake

Make a nice little cake. Add strained carrots.

This is the method Grandmother B.'s Orange cake gave in her church cook book printed years and years ago. It said "Make a nice little cake, and then use the following sauce over it."

Very few directions were given on these recipe cards. I am not sure where my mother obtained them. I found this in my mom's recipe box.

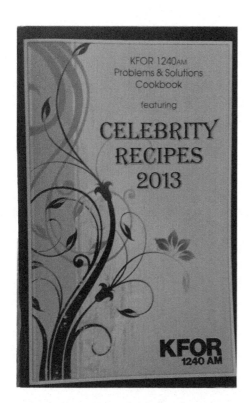

Old Cookbooks

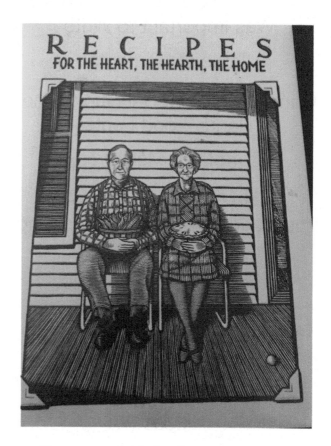

The cover of this family cookbook was done by Kathy Bitzer's cousin.

Table of Contents

Commonly Used Definitions
And
Handy Food Facts

t. , tsp. = teaspoon
T, Tbsp. = tablespoon
C. = cup
fg. = few grains
oz. = ounce or ounces
lb. = pound
sq. = square
min. = minute or minutes
hr. = hour or hours
mod. = moderate or moderately
doz. = dozen
temp. = temperature

1 kilogram = 2.205 pounds
1 sq. chocolate = 1 ounce
3 ½ Tbsp. cocoa and ½ Tbsp. butter = 1 ounce chocolate
Dash, few grains = less than 1/8 teaspoon
1 lemon = 3 to 4 Tbsp. juice
Grated peel of lemon = 1 ½ teaspoon
1 1/3 Tbsp. vinegar or 1 ½ Tbsp. lemon juice and sweet milk = 1 cup sour milk

Simplified Measures

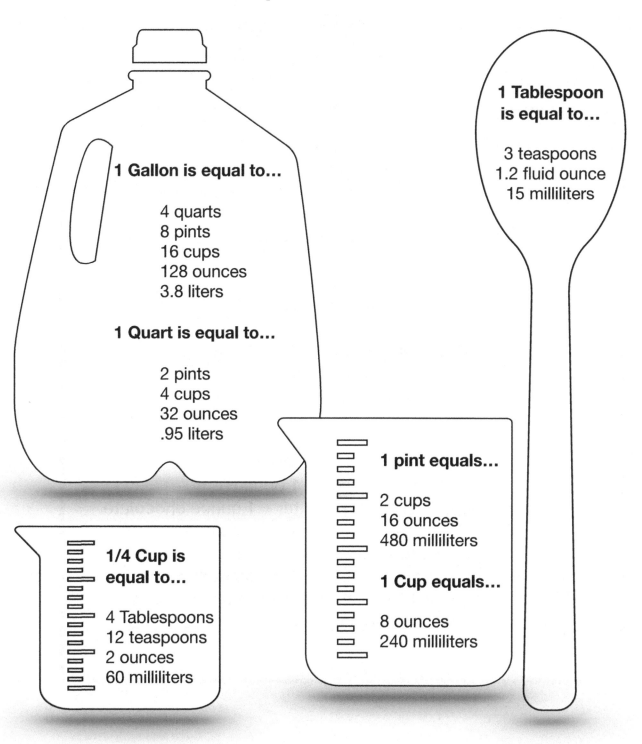

1 Gallon is equal to...

4 quarts
8 pints
16 cups
128 ounces
3.8 liters

1 Quart is equal to...

2 pints
4 cups
32 ounces
.95 liters

1 Tablespoon is equal to...

3 teaspoons
1.2 fluid ounce
15 milliliters

1 pint equals...

2 cups
16 ounces
480 milliliters

1 Cup equals...

8 ounces
240 milliliters

1/4 Cup is equal to...

4 Tablespoons
12 teaspoons
2 ounces
60 milliliters

Let The Celebration Begin!

Appetizers, Beverages, Dips, and Salad Dressings

In Redd Griffin's review of "Hemingway on food: Eating to live and living to eat" (Oak Park.com, Nov. 8, 2005) he says that Hemingway's memoir, *A Moveable Feast*, "is more than getting, preparing, and consuming food. It is about the people, the events, the ambience, and the meaning of his early years in Paris."

The gathering of these recipes made me think that they are all about the people, events, the ambience, and meaning or memories associated with the dish.

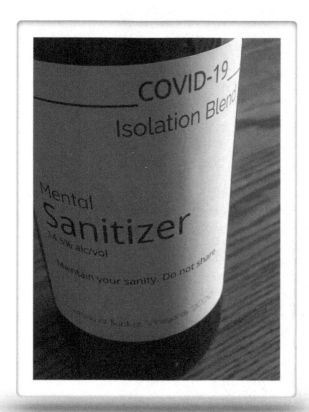

Bob Bitzer's COVID-19 Isolation blend
wine bottle

Memories of wine on the river!

Gougers' (French cheese puff appetizers)
Bev Austin

This is my favorite recipe when someone says "Bring something." It's pretty much foolproof if you follow the directions and don't over beat the batter. People gobble these down as appetizers with wine or their drink of choice.

Step One
2/3 C milk
½ C water
4 T unsalted butter, in four chunks
¼ t salt
Dash cayenne pepper
Dash nutmeg
1 C all-purpose flour

Bring milk, water, butter, salt, cayenne & nutmeg to a boil in saucepan. Remove from heat, add flour all at once, and mix vigorously with a wooden spoon until mixture forms a ball. Return pan to heat and cook over medium heat, stirring occasionally, for about 1 minute to dry the mixture a bit. Transfer to bowl of food processor, let cool for 5 minutes, then process for about 5 seconds.

Step Two
3 large eggs (room temperature)
¼ t paprika

Add eggs and paprika to the processor bowl and process for 10 to 15 seconds, until well-mixed. Transfer the choux paste to a mixing bowl and let cool for 10 minutes.

Step Three
2 C grated Gruyere or Emmenthaler cheese (or 1 ½ C of one of these + ½ C Parmesan cheese)
1 T finely grated Parmesan cheese
Fleur de sel for sprinkling

Line 2 cookie sheets with Silpat or parchment paper. Add 2 C cheese to choux paste and stir just enough to incorporate. Using a tablespoon, scoop out a level tablespoon of gouger dough and push it off the spoon onto the cooking mat (note: I just used a 1 T miniature ice cream scoop). Continue making individual gougeres, spacing them about 2 inches apart on the sheet. Sprinkle a few grains of fleur de sel and a tiny bit of Parmesan cheese on each gouger.

Bake at 425 for 15 minutes, then turn oven down to 375 and continue baking for 10 minutes or until gougeres are a nice brown (not pale golden brown, but deeper brown). Turn oven off and remove cookie sheets. Pierce top of each gouger with a small, sharp knife. Return cookie sheets to cooling oven for 10 minutes. Remove gougers and cool completely on racks.

Note: Best served fresh. However, the books say you can freeze these separately and keep them in a plastic bag in the freezer. Instructions are to cook frozen, adding a few minutes to oven time.

Almond Stuffed Bacon Wrapped Dates
Connie Hirz

These have become a favorite appetizer for gatherings as they are assembled ahead of time and are so delicious. The recipe comes from The Seasoned Chef Cooking School, Chef Shellie Kark, Denver, CO.

Ingredients
24 Medjool dates, pitted
24 Marcona almonds
8 thin slices bacon

Instructions
Preheat oven to 350 degrees.
Stuff each date with a whole almond.
Cut each strip of bacon into three pieces. Gently wrap a bacon piece around each date, overlapping back so that it adheres to itself. Use a toothpick to pierce through the layers of bacon and the date. Place wrapped dates on a parchment lined cookie sheet. Chill in refrigerator at least 10 minutes or overnight before baking.

Place the dates into the preheated oven and bake until the fat is rendered and the bacon is crisp—about 12-15 minutes. Remove from oven and serve warm or room temperature.

Yield 24 pieces

Bacon Roll-ups
Mark Onstott

This is an appetizer that we have a tradition of making for New Year's Eve and special occasions. It was handed down from my mom who always made it for New Year's Eve as well. We like to keep the tradition.

Ingredients
½ C sour cream
½ t onion salt
½ lb. bacon – cooked and crumbled
10 oz. package crescent rolls

Instructions
Separate rolls. Mix all the ingredients and spread on the crescent rolls. Cut rolls into thirds and roll up. Bake at 375 for 12-15 minutes.

Tony and Luigi's Cheese Spread
Fran Colon

If you lived in Lincoln, Nebraska, you probably went to Tony and Luigi's to eat some of the best Italian food around! This cheese spread was served before your meal and was relished by everyone. Tony and Luigi's restaurant closed several years ago, but I found this in an old cookbook as I was sorting through my cookbook collection and I wanted to share.

Ingredients
8 oz. cream cheese
1 pkg. onion soup
18 oz. cottage cheese
3 T Worcestershire sauce

Instructions
Blend with mixer. Chill for 6 hours before serving with crackers or vegetables.

Marilyn's Crab Dip
Cari Southerland

My first job out of college was 1,000 miles from "home," and one of the Admins at the office adopted me. This recipe is her signature that was always on the table at every work potluck, party, and event we went to. When I moved back to Colorado, Marilyn gave me the recipe, along with a container of dip for the road!

Ingredients
1 can crab meat
1 8 oz. brick cream cheese
1 can of cream of mushroom soup
1 packet gelatin
1 stalk celery, diced small
2 green onions, diced small

Instructions
Microwave the cream cheese and soup together for 2 minutes and stir. DO NOT BOIL.
Add remainder of ingredients and stir all together.
Refrigerate for at least I hour. Serve with crackers or pita chips.

Chicken Wing Dip
Kristin Dulany

I usually make this as a Super Bowl snack because it is a favorite. One day I happened to make it on a non-Super Bowl day. My youngest daughter, Kaycee, came downstairs and asked if the Super Bowl was on. Clearly you can make it other times of the year and it is a success.

Ingredients
1 C shredded, canned, or rotisserie chicken
2 C shredded Colby Jack cheese
½ C Franks hot sauce
½ C Ranch dressing
1 (8 oz.) brick of softened cream cheese

Instructions
Mix together. Bake at 350 for 20-25 minutes.

Holiday Cheese Ball
Anne White

This has been an annual Christmas gift from Pege, a good friend from work. We always looked forward to it and always appreciated it.

Ingredients

2 8 oz. pkg. cream cheese
1 8 ½ oz. can crushed pineapple – well drained
2 C chopped pecans
1 T seasoned salt
¼ C chopped green pepper
2 T chopped onions

Instructions

Let cream cheese stand at room temperature to soften. Mix in pineapple. When smooth, add 1 cup pecans, green pepper, onion, and seasoned salt. Chill. Form into ball and roll in remaining cup of pecans. Chill until serving time. Serve with assorted crackers.

Cheese Ball
Kathy Bitzer

My mom always made up 3 cheese balls for our Christmas gathering. Everyone knew "Millie" would be bringing them for our large gathering (56 cousins) and 20 adults.

Ingredients
8 oz. cream cheese
2.5 oz. pkg dried beef
Green onion tops
1 t Accent
1 t Worcestershire

Instructions
Mix softened cream cheese, the tops of the green onions, chopped up (dried beef), Accent, and Worcestershire. Mix well and form into a ball. Chill for at least 2 hours. Can be made the day before as well. This cracker dip is a great hit with all ages.

Vegetable Dip
Virginia White

We were frequently invited to play cards at a friend's house when we lived in Cheyenne, Wyoming. I'm not sure who brought this dip, but it was great to munch on while playing cards. Because I love cheese, I loved the combination of that with the other ingredients. You can use it with crackers as well, but we loved it with a variety of veggies.

Ingredients
1 ½ C sour cream
1 C shredded cheddar cheese (we like sharp)
¼ C finely chopped onion
3 T minced green pepper
¼ t salt
1/8 t Tabasco
1 T milk (add more if necessary)

Instructions
Mix all ingredients. Cover and refrigerate for at least 1 hour before serving.

Olga's Deviled Eggs
Cheryl L. Ilov

Olga was my mom's best friend for forty years. They met when my oldest sister and Olga's eldest son started kindergarten together. Not only did Olga and my mom become great friends, so did our families, and we spent a tremendous amount of time together. Which is interesting, since Olga and her husband had three boys and my mom and dad had five girls, but we all got along quite well together, and even went on vacations together a few times.

Both sets of parents are gone now, and Olga's boys and my sisters are scattered across the country, but we still keep in touch. This recipe is to celebrate life, love, and lasting friendship. To this day I can't look a deviled egg in the eye without thinking of Olga, her family, and the good times we shared over the years.

Ingredients
6 hard boiled eggs, chilled and peeled
¼ C mayonnaise
1 t vinegar
1 t prepared mustard
¼ t salt
Dash of black pepper
Optional: paprika, parsley, sliced black olives

Instructions
Cut the chilled and peeled eggs in half lengthwise. Remove the yolks and place in a small bowl, crushing them thoroughly with a fork and set aside. In a small bowl, combine the other ingredients and mix well, then add the yolks. Mix well.

Stuff the egg whites with the yolk mixture, arranging them on a serving plate. Garnish the eggs with parsley, paprika, and/or even a slice of black olive.

Red Sangria
Cari Southerland

Years ago we played Flyball with our dogs. For those who aren't familiar, Flyball is a relay race with teams of 4 dogs—they run over 4 jumps, get a ball from the box, and run back. Anyway, Flyball tournaments are all day affairs—just hanging out with friends, dogs, food, and drink!

We pulled this recipe together because we had a lot of wine, and wanted something we could mix together and enjoy at the Flyball tournaments. It's become a summer staple—served at picnics, pool parties, or just hanging out on our deck. This recipe is super easy to double, which we often did when taking it to a tournament! You could really add any fruit to it that you like, but this combination always came out perfect!

Ingredients
1 bottle red wine
½ C brandy
½ C orange juice
1 ¼ T granulated sugar (to taste) *note (if sweeter wine is chosen, mix everything first, and then add sugar a bit at a time)
1 sliced orange
1 sliced lemon
1 sliced lime
1 sliced peach (or canned peaches)
1 C club soda

Instructions
Mix together in a pitcher. Serve over ice.

"Take another glass of wine, and excuse my mentioning that society as a body does not expect one to be so strictly conscientious in emptying one's glass, as to turn it bottom upwards with the rim on one's nose."
Great Expectations
Charles Dickens

Very Berry Zinger Punch
Rosette Obedoza

The original source of this potluck favorite is unknown, but one of my mother's friends shared this recip̶ during a family picnic. Children in the family opt for this refreshing drink during birthday parties. A good number of adults also gravitate toward this beverage during the summer birthday parties that are usually held outdoors, often in the parks. A crowd pleaser, for sure!

Ingredients

1 small package strawberry Kool-Aid
1 small package cherry Kool-Aid
2 C sugar
2 quarts water
1 large can frozen orange juice
1 large can frozen lemonade
1 bottle soda water
1 half gallon raspberry sherbet

Instructions

Mix Kool-Aids, sugar, water, orange juice, and lemonade. Chill. At serving time add soda water and sherbet by the scoop. Stir just to blend.

Crockpot Hot Chocolate
Marilyn Ferguson

This is the hot chocolate that we always serve at church after our Christmas program. It's a big hit with children and adults.

Ingredients
3 C cream
2 cans sweetened condensed milk
12 C milk
2 t Vanilla
4 C milk chocolate chips

Instructions
Stir together cream, condensed milk, milk, and vanilla in crockpot.
Melt the chocolate chips and then mix into milk.
Put on high until very warm, then turn on warm to keep ready for family and friends.

Maple Cider Vinaigrette
Larry Johnston

On one of our past Thanksgiving dinners, a person preparing the salads knew that I wasn't a salad lover. She made it her goal to make sure that I enjoyed her salad selection without letting anyone else know she was preparing this surprise salad recipe for me. When I took a smaller serving to show my appreciation for all our cooks, she was specifically watching my response. When other conversations were going on, she heard me say, "WOW!" I told her this was more like a dessert than a salad as I was loading my plate with an additional serving. She was pleased and wanted to make sure I enjoyed a salad and not just the meats.

Ingredients for the Vinaigrette
1/3 C cider vinegar
2 T pure maple syrup
1 T dijon mustard
¼ t kosher salt
¼ t ground pepper
2/3 C olive oil

Ingredients for the Salad
10 oz. pkg. baby spinach
1 Gala apple thinly sliced
4 oz. crumbled goat cheese
¼ C crushed pecans

Instructions
To prepare vinaigrette, whisk together cider vinegar and all ingredients without the olive oil. After all ingredients are mixed together well, gradually whisk in the olive oil until all is well blended.

Pour desired amount on your salad and you'll think dessert has been served!

A Glaze for All Seasons
Jennifer Condreay

I have called this glaze many things: Jenny Ling's (referring to me) or I-Would-Have-To-Kill-You-If-I-Gave-You-the-Recipe Asian Glaze, or Liquid Gold. Truth is, Williams Sonoma was the spot where I bought this for years. When I went one day to restock my supply, the sales person told me that the company no longer carried that product Ah! I used this for a dipping sauce for vegetables, a glaze over roasted salmon or chicken, the base for any stir fry dish, or in a vinaigrette for Asian salads. It was a staple in my kitchen. That day, I was determined to duplicate my own brew and studied the label of the empty bottle. I travelled all over Denver to wonderful Asian grocery stores to find the rare ingredients, but over the years have found that they all can be purchased at most grocery stores. I think the influence is mostly Korean and that people will love this sweet, hot, spicy sauce. Enjoy!

Ingredients

1 8 oz. bottle of sweet chili sauce

3 T sesame oil

3 T soy sauce

3 T Fermented Black Bean Paste (It might not say "fermented" on the bottle. I cannot even duplicate the Korean spelling of it!)

1 T fish sauce

1 T brown sugar

1 T Sriracha sauce

2 T orange marmalade

Instructions

If glaze is stored in an airtight jar, it lasts in the fridge for two months. If you "can" it and seal it, it last indefinitely.

Gather Around For The Feast

Entrees

"I can't stand people who do not take food seriously."
Oscar Wilde

Gluten Free Pasta

Thick Crust Sicilian Paleo Pizza

Country Chicken Casserole
Jeannine Green

This is kind of a funny story. My husband Jay and I were high-school sweethearts. We started dating in 1976. I used to think my mother was a good cook until Jay and I started dating and I began hanging out at his family dinners. Jay's mother, Ester Green, came from a line of German descendants. She and her nine siblings were used to scrumptious cooking thanks to their mother who was also named Ester. Now I'm not saying that my dear Swedish mother couldn't cook, it's just that she gave birth to me after my brothers were raised and had left home; she said she was tired of cooking! I must say, though, that lemon pies were her "specialty."

The following two recipes were shared time and time again at the "Green" family gatherings.

Ingredients
3 lbs. (or less) chicken
¼ C flour
¼ C chopped green pepper
3 sliced (1 inch) carrots
3 sliced (1 inch) celery stalks
¼ C (or more) chopped onion
1 clove garlic (or more), minced
1 ½ C large macaroni

Instructions
Sprinkle chicken with flour, salt, and pepper to taste. Brown in skillet. Remove chicken from pan. In the same pan, sauté lightly onion, pepper, and garlic. Add remaining ingredients EXCEPT macaroni and simmer 10 minutes. Put uncooked macaroni in greased casserole dish. Cover with chicken. Pour skillet mixture over all. Cover and bake at 350 for 1-1 ½ hours or until chicken and vegetables are tender. Yummy! (Recipe is flexible).

Chicken Delight
Jeannine Green

Ingredients

2- 2 ½ lbs. chicken
Seasoned flour (enough for dredging the chicken)
Oil for browning the chicken
2 T Worcestershire sauce
1 large onion sliced
1 green pepper sliced
1 can mushrooms
2 T molasses
¼ t paprika
1 C catsup
¼ t salt

Instructions

Wash then roll chicken in seasoned flour. Brown the chicken in a skillet in hot fat. Then place the chicken in a 2 qt casserole.

Sauté onions, pepper, and mushrooms in butter until tender. Add remaining ingredients PLUS 2/3 C water and bring to boil. Pour over chicken in casserole. Cover and bake 45 minutes at 325.

(Recipe is flexible. You can use red pepper, olive oil instead of butter, etc.) Hope you enjoy!

Chicken and Dressing
Elaine Michaud

This is a favorite of my family in the fall. I found the recipe in the Elwood United Methodist Church cookbook that my sister-in-law, Gayle Cooksley, sent me in 1987.

Ingredients
½ C chopped onion
1 stick oleo (1/4 C)
½ C chopped celery
8 oz. seasoned stuffing mix
3 C diced chicken
1 C broth
½ C mayonnaise
½ t salt
2 eggs
1 ½ C milk
1 can cream of mushroom soup

Instructions
Brown onion and celery in oleo. Mix together stuffing mix, chicken, broth, celery, onion, oleo, and put half of mix in greased 9 x 13 inch pan. Combine mayonnaise and salt. Spread over first half of mix in pan. Put rest of chicken mix on top. Beat eggs and add to milk. Pour over mix in pan. Cover with foil. Refrigerate overnight. One hour before baking, spread 1 can mushroom soup over dressing. Bake at 325 for 40-50 minutes. This can be frozen before heating. Yummy in the tummy!

Poule Merd
(Traditional French country recipe - "Chicken in a Pot")
Elaine Michaud

Years ago when my kids were young and very picky eaters, I made up a casserole with food that they would eat and could be put in the oven while we watched the Super Bowl. When it was just about ready for the oven, Michelle looked at it and asked what it was. I just said "some chicken stuff." She looked at it and said, "It looks like chicken s**t to me." Eventually this casserole turned out to be a family favorite and when asked for – we all use her words. However, in our family cookbook, we use the French name.

Ingredients
2 to 2 ½ C cooked rice
1 can cream of chicken soup
1 small jar Cheez Whiz
1 soup can milk
4 chicken breasts, cooked
1 C corn flake crumbs
¼ C melted butter

Instructions
Stir soup, Cheez Whiz, and milk into rice. Add diced chicken. Pour into 9 x 13 casserole dish. Mix corn flake crumbs with melted butter and spread on top. Bake at 350 for 30-35 minutes.

Chicken and Mushrooms
Gaspar Sabater

These two recipes are two of my favorites because my mother used to cook them for my brother and me. We usually ate them during the winter time, but there were special requests during summer times also. My wife prepares these dishes almost in the same way as my mother did. So I guess it's all about the love and dedication that people we care about and put into cooking these delicious meals for us.

Ingredients
1 whole chicken, cut up
2 onions, sliced
1 sweet pepper, sliced
A half glass of white wine
1 kilogram of potatoes
3 T oil
Spices (Gaspar says they use pepper, salt, barley, cinnamon, chili to taste)
Champignon mushrooms (button mushrooms)

Instructions
Put a big pot on the stove, add 3 T oil. Add the chicken and cook for ten minutes. Cut the onion and sweet pepper into slices, add them inside the pot and mix with chicken. Cook for 20 more minutes. Add the half glass of wine, leave the pot without the lid so the alcohol evaporates and flavor remains. Add different spices to taste. Finally add the sliced mushrooms and keep cooking for another 20 minutes.

Peel and dice the potatoes. Fry them with oil in a frying pan. Serve on a big platter all together.

Potato Pie
Gaspar Sabater

Ingredients

1 kilogram of chopped meat (Gaspar said they usually use beef, but you can also use veal or pork)
2 onions, sliced
1 sweet pepper, sliced
3 eggs
2 kilograms of peeled potatoes
Sliced parmesan cheese

Instructions

Cook the sliced pepper and onions with a little oil in a frying pan for 10 minutes. Add the chopped meat and the spices and salt to your pleasure. Meanwhile boil the potatoes and the eggs. Once that is done, mash the potatoes and mix with the hard boiled eggs.

After that, put it all in an oven glass dish following this order. First put about half of the mashed potatoes covering the entire dish, then add the meat on top and then the pepper and onions. Cover the top surface with the rest of the mashed potatoes and sprinkle with the sliced parmesan. Put the dish in the oven and cook at 250 for 25 minutes.

Parmesan Chicken
Kathi Emery Vontz

This recipe comes from my daughter and has been a favorite.

Ingredients
½ C butter or margarine, melted
2 t Dijon mustard
1 t Worcestershire Sauce
½ t salt
1 C dry bread crumbs
½ C grated Parmesan cheese
6-8 boneless, skinless chicken breasts

Instructions
In a pie plate or shallow bowl, combine butter, mustard, Worcestershire sauce and salt. In a plastic bag, combine crumbs and Parmesan cheese. Dip chicken in butter mixture, then shake in crumb mixture. Place in ungreased 13 x 9 x2 baking pan. Drizzle with any remaining butter mixture. Bake at 350 for 40-45 minutes or until chicken is no longer pink and juices run clear. Yield: 6-8 servings

Crockpot Chicken Roll-ups
Virginia White

I discovered this recipe when I was teaching in Cheyenne. The crockpot became a good friend when I spent so much time preparing lessons, grading papers, attending meetings, and running the girls to music and athletic activities. As with all discovered recipes, you eventually learn to adjust a few things to meet your desires. This recipe has become a family favorite and is requested again and again.

Ingredients

3 whole skinned and boned chicken breasts
6 small slices of thin sliced ham
6 small slices of Swiss cheese
¼ C flour
¼ C Kraft grated Parmesan Cheese or a blend – I usually use more cheese than flour
1 t salt
½ t pepper
½ t powdered sage
1/3 C oil
1 can condensed cream of chicken soup
½ C dry white wine or chicken broth

Instructions

Cut each breast in half; pound to make thin. Place a slice of ham and cheese on each piece of chicken. Roll the combination up. Tuck ends in and secure with a toothpick. Dip chicken roll-ups in flour, Parmesan, salt, sage, and pepper mixture. Save any left- over mixture. Chill chicken at least an hour (You can skip this if you need to) Heat oil and sauté chicken on all sides. Place browned chicken in crockpot. Add soup mixed with wine or broth. Cook 4-5 hours on high. Remove chicken and thicken broth with left-over flour mixture. Serve over rice.

Chicken-Stuffed shells with Two Sauces
Virginia White

After Mom died, we traveled to Nebraska often and I always tried to find something new to cook for Dad. He bought a little recipe book and thought he would be able to make some of the things in it. When I looked at him and the book, I knew that probably wouldn't be a good idea. I found this idea in the book and changed a few things to fit his tastes. It has become a family favorite and something my grandkids request all of the time. Since then, I have found a variety of recipes similar to this one.

Ingredients
18 uncooked jumbo pasta shells
¾ C lightly packed chopped fresh basil leaves OR dried basil leaves to taste
1 large can of chicken – drain the broth (I usually save it for another chicken recipe)
1 C small-curd cottage cheese or Ricotta
1 egg
2 C pasta sauce of choice
1 container (10 oz) refrigerated Alfredo sauce
½ C grated Parmesan cheese (I usually use more)

Instructions
Heat oven to 350. Spray 13 x 9 (3 quart) glass baking dish with cooking spray. Cook and drain pasta shells as directed on package. In medium bowl, mix ½ C of the basil leaves or dried basil, the chicken, cottage cheese or Ricotta, and egg. I add additional Parmesan cheese to the mix.

Pour pasta sauce into baking dish, spread to evenly coat bottom of dish. Spoon about 1 heaping tablespoon mixture into each cooked pasta shell. Place filled shells over sauce, filled sides up. Drizzle Alfredo sauce over shells. Add additional basil if desired. Sprinkle with Parmesan cheese. Cover tightly with foil.

Bake 35 to 40 minutes or until sauce is bubbly and shells are hot. I usually take the foil off and bake it another 15-20 minutes.

Chicken Tortilla Casserole
Bob and Kathy Bitzer

This has been a hit with our family because everyone down to the grandkids enjoy it!

Ingredients

1 whole chicken or 4 large chicken breasts
4 chicken bouillon cubes
1 C water
2 cans cream of chicken soup
½ onion, chopped
1 small can chopped green chilies
¼ C jalapeños
8 oz. cheddar cheese
½ C sour cream
6-8 flour tortillas

Instructions

Cook chicken and cut into bite size pieces. Mix bouillon cubes in 1 cup water and dissolve. Mix chicken, soup, onion, bouillon, chilies, jalapeños. Tear enough tortillas to cover the bottom of a greased 9x13 pan Start layering – tortillas, chicken mixture and top with cheddar cheese. Continue to layer the ingredients. Finish with cheese. Bake at 350 for 45 minutes. Serve with lettuce, tomato, and sour cream.

Grandma Cederdahl's Mock Chicken Loaf
Janet Grabenstein

My cousin Donna was raised by my grandparents and always took her lunch to school when she was young. She didn't care for beef, especially ground beef. So, the improvisation took place to make her think it was chicken vs meat loaf in her sandwiches. Plus, the "thing" at that time was using Campbell soup in recipes. It is soft when used hot and delicious when used cold in sandwiches.

Ingredients
1 lb. ground beef
1 beaten egg
2 C dry bread crumbs
2 cans Campbell Chicken Noodle Soup, mashed by running it through a blender
1 small onion
1/8 t pepper
½ t salt
½ t each sage and poultry seasoning
1 C milk

Instructions
Preheat oven to 350.
Mix together all of the ingredients and form it into a loaf.
Bake at 350 for 1 hour.

Grilled Beef Tenderloin
Don Spinar

Steak on the grill just tastes better since the meat juice drips on the coals and smokes the meat for more flavor. This will serve four normal people or less for big eaters. Whenever I do this, we normally get three meals out of it including great sandwiches. Sometimes I put horseradish on the side for dipping or on bread for a sandwich. It is best to let the meat rest for 10 minutes after taking off the grill.

Ingredients
2 lbs of beef tenderloin in a single piece
8 slices of bacon (more if needed to wrap around the tenderloin)
Salt
Pepper
Beef Seasoning of choice

Instructions
Trim fat off of the tenderloin. Wrap about 8 slices of bacon around the meat, securing with toothpicks. Season with salt and pepper or Misty's beef seasoning or any other beef seasoning.

Cook for 30-40 minutes at about 350, turning every 10 minutes.

I seldom use a meat thermometer but about 140 degrees will be medium. Less time if you want it more rare. I use the "feel" test. If the meat is somewhat firm, then it is probably done.

The bacon flares up so it is wise to cook with the grill lid down. Have a water bottle ready if it flames. It won't hurt the meat.

Barbecued Beef Sandwiches
Lauren Sternburg

In 1979, when faced with a horde of friends coming to my home to watch the Washington Redskins and armed without any cooking skills, I turned to *Marlene Sorosky's Cookery for Entertaining.* There I found a recipe for brisket sandwiches that was a huge hit and I have altered it for special occasions for the past three decades.

I suggest Kaiser rolls for the sandwiches. If you don't have a lemon to slice, forget about it. No worries, it still tastes great. Same goes for the liquid smoke, nice addition, but not necessary. You can even forget the rolls and just serve the sliced brisket as the main course for a sit-down dinner. Not only does it taste great, but it can be made ahead of time.

After having the brisket for many Sabbath dinners, our older son called it "Friday meat" and it was the first thing he asked for when our family moved to Colorado.

Ingredients

1 4-5 pound brisket
Salt and pepper to taste
2 8 oz. cans tomato sauce
½ C water
½ C chopped onion
1 garlic clove, minced
¼ C red wine vinegar
1 T Worcestershire sauce
1/3 C brown sugar, firmly packed
2 T honey
2 t dried mustard
1 t chili powder
1 t salt
1 small lemon, thinly sliced
Dash liquid smoke if desired

Instructions

Sprinkle brisket with salt and pepper. Preheat oven to 325. Place roast in covered roasting pan for 3 to 4 hours until tender when pierced with a fork. Cook and then refrigerate.

Mix remaining ingredients in a medium sauce pan. Bring to a boil. Lower heat and simmer uncovered for 30 minutes, stirring occasionally and set aside.

Cut excess fat from beef. Slice meat into thin slices. Place a layer of meat in a large oven-to-table casserole dish. Spread with a layer of sauce. Continue layering meat and sauce until all is used. Cover with foil. May be refrigerated for up to three days or frozen.

Before serving sandwiches, bring meat and sauce to room temperature. Preheat oven to 350. Bake 1 hour, until heated through. Serve with assorted sandwich rolls if desired. Makes 10-12 servings.

Barbecue Beef Kabobs
Garrett Dulany

I love new foods, so last year I took a cooking class to see what I could discover about foods and my ability to make the dishes. I really liked what I made in class because I had to do everything by hand and it was nice to see what type of food I was capable of making. The kabobs I made in class were a favorite of mine. I couldn't find the exact recipe I made in class, so I found one created for Taste of Home that was very close to the one I made in class. I loved the finished product!

Ingredients
1 C ketchup
1/3 C French salad dressing
1/3 C reduced-sodium soy sauce
1 T Worcestershire sauce
1 pound boneless beef sirloin steak, cut into 1 inch cubes
1 C fresh baby carrots
2 T water
1 pound medium fresh mushrooms, halved
1 medium green pepper, cut into 1 inch pieces
½ medium onion, cut into 1 inch pieces
Hot cooked rice, optional

Instructions
In a small bowl, combine the ketchup, salad dressing, soy sauce, and Worcestershire sauce. Transfer 1/3 cup to another bowl for basting; cover and refrigerate.

Pour remaining marinade into a large resealable plastic bag; add steak. Seal bag and turn to coat. Make sure steak is well covered with marinade. Refrigerate for at least an hour.

Place carrots and water in a microwave-safe dish on high for 4 minutes. Drain and discard marinade.

You can use metal or soaked wooden skewers and alternately thread the beef and vegetables.

You can also vary vegetables if you want to try something different.

Grill, covered, over medium-hot heat for 10-20 minutes until meat reaches the desired doneness, basting frequently with reserved marinade and turning once. The less time grilled, the more rare the beef.

We liked this with rice, but you could certainly serve this alone or another side dish of your choice.

Brisket
Dawn Vaughn

My mom used to make this recipe every time the family gathered. Once Mother stated that she just couldn't cook Thanksgiving dinner anymore, and my nephew asked, "But can you still make the brisket?" Clearly a favorite.

Ingredients
10-12 lb brisket (trimmed)
Celery salt
Garlic salt
Liquid smoke
½ C Worcestershire sauce

Instructions
Poke holes in brisket with a fork. Liberally sprinkle both sides of the meat with celery salt and garlic salt. Add liquid smoke and rub in well with hands. Wrap in foil and marinate 1-2 days in the fridge, turning several times.

To cook, remove foil and place fat side down in 3 qt. rectangular casserole dish. Add Worcestershire sauce over the top of the brisket. Cover tightly with foil. Cook in 275 degree oven overnight or 6-7 hours. Do NOT overcook. Let stand before slicing the meat against the grain only.

Place broth in a bowl, cover, and refrigerate. After broth is cold, skim the fat off the top and pour over brisket. Can freeze or refrigerate.

You can cook the brisket the day before serving and refrigerate it and broth separately. Then slice it and pour broth over it and heat in the oven.

Eyeball Casserole OR
Meatball Sub Casserole
Judy Kenna

I started making this casserole years ago for my grandchildren and their parents on Halloween before the entire crew headed out to trick or treat. My grandchildren enjoyed the fact that the meatballs can be made to look like eyeballs with well placed mozzarella cheese. It is now known as eyeball casserole and it is our traditional Halloween dinner.

Ingredients

1 bag frozen meatballs – defrosted
1 loaf (1 pound) of French bread cut into 1 inch cubes
2 (8 oz.) packages of softened cream cheese
1 C mayonnaise
1 C shredded mozzarella cheese
1 jar spaghetti sauce
1 t Italian seasoning
1 C water
2 garlic cloves minced

Instructions

Arrange bread cubes in a greased 13x 9 pan. Combine cream cheese, mayo, Italian seasoning and pepper. Spread over bread. Sprinkle with 1 cup Mozzarella cheese. Combine spaghetti sauce, water, and garlic. Add meatballs and pour sauce with meatballs over cheese mixture. Then, top with remaining Mozzarella cheese and bake at 350 degrees for 45 minutes.

Mom's Cold Winter Dinner Treat
Beth McCane

This was a favorite because my mom pretty much only made it on really cold winter nights. Coming inside from shoveling snow and smelling it simmer just made my dad and me melt. It took the chill right out of our bones.

Ingredients
1 to 1 ½ lbs hamburger
1 green bell pepper, diced
1 onion, diced
1 C elbow macaroni
1 1 lb. can stewed tomatoes
Bay leaf (optional)
Basil (optional)

Instructions
Thoroughly cook the hamburger adding in diced green bell peppers and onions. Drain off all of the fat. Add stewed tomatoes and simmer for about 15 minutes. You can add bay leaf and basil to taste if desired to the mix during the simmer. While the mixture is simmering, cook about 1 C of elbow macaroni and drain. When the hamburger mixture is done add it to the cooked macaroni.

Serve with dinner roll

Easy Beef Roast
Kathi Emery Vontz

This is so simple, yet versatile. I use it mostly to shred and add BBQ sauce for the easiest BBQ beef sandwiches. I also slice it sometimes for cold roast beef sandwiches or grind it up for beef salad sandwiches (an oldie but goodie). I found this years ago in the Nebraska First Ladies cookbook. I think you might say it is my "go-to" recipe for sandwiches.

Place roast (any quality) in a covered pan at 350 for 15 minutes. Reduce heat to 200 for 8-10 hours. Use no water or seasonings. It will be delicious. When it is cold, it is excellent – moist and easy to cut.

Piccadillo Pork Burritos
Dede Stockton

This has been a family favorite for years! We love Mexican food and the pork and spices in this burrito make this the most tender burrito you have ever eaten! The cinnamon gives the dish a unique flavor that is hard to surpass. It is my go to meal whenever I happen to have a pork tenderloin in the freezer. All of us enjoy them immensely!

Ingredients

1 lb pork tenderloin, trimmed and cut into ½ inches pieces
1 t Durkee ground cumin seed, or other brand
¼ t table salt
¼ t ground cinnamon
1 t vegetable oil
1 small onion, chopped
2 clove(s) garlic, minced (medium)
2/3 C salsa, or picante sauce
1/3 C queso aejo Mexican cheese, shredded
1 T cilantro, fresh, chopped
4 medium whole wheat tortilla(s)

Instructions

Place pork in a large bowl. Sprinkle with cumin, salt, and cinnamon; toss well.

Heat oil in a large skillet over medium heat. Add onion and garlic, cook 3 minutes; stir occasionally. Add pork mixture; cook 2 minutes, stirring often. Add salsa. Simmer over low heat 5 minutes or until pork loses its pink color and sauce is thick. Remove from heat; stir in cheese and cilantro.

Heat tortillas according to package directions. Spoon ¾ cup pork mixture onto each tortilla; roll up. Yield 4 servings or 4 burritos.

"And, most dear actors, eat no onions, or garlic, for we are to utter sweet breath. . ."
A Midsummer Night's Dream, Act 4 , scene 2
William Shakespeare

Chicken and Pork Adobo
Rosette Obedoza

The traditional recipe from the Philippines was handed down to me by my paternal grandmother. She raised me as a young child and has influenced me in many ways. Enjoying the art of cooking authentic Filipino recipes is one of the many ways her influence has touched me.

Ingredients
1 C vinegar
1 head garlic, crushed
10 pcs. peppercorn, crushed
1 bay leaf (dried)
2 T rock salt
4 T soy sauce
1 kg chicken, cut into serving pieces
½ kg pork, cut into 1 inch by 2 inch pieces
1 ½-2 C water
½ T liver spread
2 T canola cooking oil for frying

Instructions
In a saucepan, combine vinegar, garlic, crushed peppercorn, bay leaf, rock salt, and soy sauce. Put in chicken and pork. Let soak for 30 minutes to 1 hour. Add water and simmer uncovered until tender. Strain sauce. Add ½ T of liver spread and set aside.

Heat canola cooking oil and brown garlic and meat pieces. Pour the sauce (mixed liver spread) you set aside earlier. Stir once. Cover and simmer until sauce thickens.

Pasta Recipes for Dad
Virginia White

More cooking for Dad after Mom died. When we went to visit, I always tried to cook something for him that was a little more healthy than anything he fixed for himself. He was tempted to eat frozen meals and maybe not eat anything that was close to a healthy meal. I found the following recipes and changed them a bit to work for him and both were declared a success.

Pasta and Fresh Vegetables in Blue Cheese Sauce

Ingredients
½ lb. small pasta
1 C tomatoes, diced
½ C zucchini (I usually diced one small one)
½ C yellow squash (I diced one small one)
¼ C red pepper (you can easily add more to taste)
¼ C green pepper (you can easily add more to taste)
¼ C red wine vinegar
¼ C olive oil
1 t Italian seasoning (again decide what works to taste)
4 oz. crumbled blue cheese

Instructions
Combine all ingredients in a large glass dish. Heat in 350 oven for 30 minutes. We LOVE this and I frequently make it when fresh vegetable are easily available.

Pasta, Chicken, and Fresh Vegetables
Virginia White

Ingredients

8 oz. Farfalle or other small pasta

2½ T olive oil

2 T Mrs. Dash Garlic and Herb Seasoning Blend.

Chopped red pepper to taste. (I used about ½ C)

Chopped yellow pepper to taste (I used about ½ C)

3 cups chopped asparagus

1 C corn (if desired)

Vegetables - I add carrots, green beans, and onions from our garden if we have them. You can really add the vegetables you like.

1 large can chicken – use fork to "shred" it, reserve broth

½ C lemon juice

¾ C (or to taste) shredded Parmesan/asiago cheese -- We love cheese, so I usually add more.

Instructions

Prepare pasta according to package directions.

Meanwhile, heat oil in a large skillet over medium heat. Add vegetables and Mrs. Dash Seasoning. Cook and stir until tender. Add chicken and cook about 8 minutes. Add broth as needed.

Toss together the hot vegetables and chicken with the pasta and cheeses.

Put in a large glass dish and cook 20-30 minutes at 350 until cheese is melted.

Basic Asparagus Lasagna Served on a Bed of Oven-Roast Red Pepper Puree
Katherine McIver

This recipe was inspired by one I learned from Sandra Lotti at Toscana Saporita Cooking School in Tuscany during a short internship in June 2007. Sandra used Barilla's precooked pasta sheets, frozen asparagus and cream in her béchamel. The pureed asparagus, the addition of Pecorino Romano and the use of milk in the béchamel, and the asparagus spears to decorate the top are my own, as is the thinness of the pasta sheets and the layering. I have also developed a couple of variations (see below). This might seem like a complex recipe, but it really isn't and it is so comforting and satisfying.

Using the uncooked asparagus spears covered with parmesan cheese on top of the lasagna recalls the traditional Italian manner of treating fresh asparagus—only the addition of a drizzle of extra olive oil is omitted here. This is not a heavy lasagna; replacing the cream with milk makes the béchamel lighter, while the addition of the pecorino and parmesan cheeses adds a level of richness. The extra thin sheets of pasta alternated with a thin layer of sauce make it light, delicate, and savory. The pureed asparagus adds a touch of light green to contrast with the pasta, while the white béchamel for the top accents the bright green asparagus spears and the breadcrumbs. Chopped pistachios can be substituted for the breadcrumbs topping.

The pasta sheets can be made in advance and frozen, ready to parboil when needed. Commercial pasta sheets (preferably an Italian brand like DeCecco) can be substituted for fresh, homemade pasta. Chopped herbs can be added to the fresh pasta to add color.

The soffrito and béchamel can be made ahead of time (even mixed together)—even the day before. In fact, the béchamel without the cheese can be made ahead and frozen for later use; it is always good to have some on hand. The entire dish can be assembled and refrigerated 2 or 3 hours before baking.

Serves 4-6 people; 9 x 9 baking dish; 350 degree oven for 35-40 min; prep time: about 1-1 ½ hours depending on whether or not you are using commercial pasta or making your own.

Ingredients: For the Pasta
2 large eggs, beaten
1 ¼ cups all-purpose flour (more for the counter top)
½ t sea salt

Ingredients: For the Soffrito
¼ cup extra virgin olive oil
½ medium onion, chopped fine
1 bunch green asparagus, cut into ½" pieces (save 10-12 tips of 1½ - 2" length for decorating the top)
Salt and pepper to taste

Ingredients: for béchamel

2 cups warm whole milk
5 T unsalted butter
1/3 C all-purpose flour
A pinch of sea salt
Freshly grated nutmeg to taste
½ C each grated parmesan (plus an additional ½ cup for top) and pecorino Romano

Instructions

For the pasta, place the flour on the counter top, make a well and add the two eggs and salt; slowly incorporate the flour into eggs to form a soft dough; knead on a lightly floured surface until the dough comes together; cover and let rest for about an hour.

While the pasta dough is resting, pour the extra virgin olive oil in a 10-12" sauté pan, add the chopped onion, salt, and cook over medium/medium-low heat until the onion is softened, about 5 minutes and add the chopped asparagus and continue cooking until tender, about 15 minutes. Stir from time to time as the asparagus cooks. Taste for seasoning, add the pepper. Puree about half of the mixture with a hand blender, blender, or food processor.

Now take the pasta dough and flatten it out into a rough rectangle about ½ inch thick and cut into 4-6 pieces. Using either a hand cranked pasta machine or a pasta attachment for a Kitchen Aid mixer, start rolling out one piece of pasta starting on #1; you may need to run it through 4 or 5 times and roll it in flour to keep it from sticking. Run it through until the dough is smooth and not sticky. For each of the remaining numbers, the dough will need to go through twice ending with #5 for a thin sheet of dough.

Hang the sheet on a pasta rack or a rod to dry while rolling the remainder of the pasta. Once all the dough has been rolled out, heat a large pot of water to boiling—while waiting for it to boil, cut the pasta sheets into 8 or 9" length depending on the size of your baking dish. Once the water is boiling, add a tablespoon of salt, preferably sea salt; parboil several sheets at a time just until softened about a minute or two; scoop out and put in cold water for only a couple minutes to stop the cooking process. Place the pasta sheets on a towel laid on the counter to drain. Continue this process until all the pasta has been parboiled.

Preheat oven to 350 degrees. Oil a 9 x 9 baking dish, spread about 2 tablespoons of the asparagus béchamel on the bottom, add a layer of pasta (you may need to cut it to fit); then 2-2 ½ tablespoons of asparagus béchamel; continue until all the sauce is used, ending with a layer of pasta. Top the last layer of pasta with the reserved plain béchamel, arrange the asparagus spears in a decorative pattern, sprinkle the grated parmesan on the top layer, and dust lightly with breadcrumbs (about 1/8 cup total) or with coarsely chopped pistachios (about ¼ cup)

Bake for 35-40 minutes or until the lasagna is bubbly and golden brown. Let it sit in the oven about 5 minutes before serving. On warmed dinner plates, spread a layer of the oven-roast red pepper puree—thinly in the center where the lasagna will be placed, and somewhat thicker along the edges—about a 4-5 inch oval. Cut the lasagna into 4 or 6 equal pieces and place on piece in the center of each plate.

4 pieces if it is the main dish or 6 if it will be followed by an entree

Oven-Roast Red Pepper Puree

1- large red bell pepper, roasted and peeled

1- T extra virgin olive oil

Large pinch of dry oregano and dry thyme (fresh would be better)

Salt (preferably sea salt) and pepper to taste

To roast the peppers (heat broiler), place them on a pan lined with aluminum foil; the oven rack should be in the lower third or center of oven. Place the pan with the pepper on the rack, and roast, turn them as the peel on each side puckers and browns. Once done, put the peppers in a plastic bag and let cool until they are easy to handle, peel, and seed. (note: I usually roast several at a time. They are great in a panino with some goat cheese or as an accompaniment for grilled vegetables). Puree the pepper, olive oil, herbs, salt, and pepper in a blender until smooth, and then add about ½ teaspoon of coarsely chopped capers.

Variations:

With Gorgonzola béchamel:

For the béchamel, replace the parmesan and pecorino Romano with about 3 or 4 ounces of gorgonzola dolce.

With smoked trout or smoked salmon:

In the middle layer, add about 4 ounces of smoked trout or smoked salmon. Alternatively, fennel can replace the fish, add chopped parsley.

Homemade Gluten-Free Pasta
Marisa Jones

Being raised by Sicilian parents, everything we ate was homemade. This gluten-free pasta is one of my favorites, converted from my family's original recipe. Making this pasta always brings me back to my childhood where I'd spend all day in the kitchen with my mom, hand-rolling each pasta noodle. It was a craft to pinch the dough around each bamboo stick and rolling it in my little hands to create a long macaroni noodle. When I was 12, our family took a trip to Sicily to visit my mother's family and every day, all the women gathered in the kitchen to make homemade pasta. Each style had its own distinct ingredients, flavor, shapes, and sizes. Today my sons help me make pasta and I am honored to carry on this tradition with them.

Ingredients

6 C of Garbanzo Bean flour
5 t Xanthan gum
2 T nutmeg
2 T garlic
6 cold, large eggs
7 cold, large egg yolks
4 T olive oil
2 T cold water

Instructions:

Mix together the dry ingredients and set aside. Mix together the wet ingredients. Add flour mixture and wet ingredients to an electric mixer bowl and mix well until a dough is formed. Texture should be like playdough. Add more flour or water until dough is the perfect texture.

On a wooden cutting board, sprinkle with Cassava flour. This keeps the dough from becoming sticky. Separate dough into balls and roll each ball until flat. Cut with a knife into approximately 3x5 sizes, square or triangle, doesn't have to be perfect. If using an electric mixer with a pasta attachment, follow instructions to make pasta.

For a pasta maker:

Prepare a baking sheet with plastic wrap on the bottom and sprinkle Cassava flour on the plastic wrap. Place pasta maker setting to 3 (mid-sized). Using the flat roller setting, place each dough piece into the flat roller and it should look like a lasagna noodle. If the dough comes out in pieces, knead it and roll it through again. Place the noodles on a tablecloth to dry as you finish the rest of the dough.

Once the dough is all rolled out, take each lasagna noodle and run it through the fettucine roller. This dough is fragile, so you won't be able to make spaghetti noodles. Grab the fettucine as it comes out and place it on the baking sheet. Continue until the sheet is full, then sprinkle more Cassava flour over the pasta. Place another lining of plastic wrap and Cassava flour and begin another layer of pasta. Continue until all pasta is finished.

To store, place in an airtight container and freeze. It will stay fresh for 2-3 months.

For hand rolling:

Roll dough into large logs. Cut small pieces, approximately a half-inch length. Pinch each dough piece around a bamboo stick. Roll in palm of your hands until the pasta forms a large tubular macaroni about 6-8 inches long. Pull out the bamboo stick and place pasta on the baking sheet, sprinkled with Cassava flour so it doesn't stick. Continue to do this until all of the dough is gone.

Cooking

Bring water to a rolling boil, then add pasta. Cook for 15-20 minutes. Keep checking it. If you over cook this pasta, it will start to disintegrate.

Thick Crust Sicilian Paleo Pizza
Marisa Jones

This pizza is a grain-free version of my mother's and grandmother's recipe. It's one of my favorites. I can remember spending all day in the kitchen with my mom when we would make 3 or 4 pizzas in one day. We'd start by making the pizza sauce, cooking the sausage, and adding different toppings for each. My siblings and I would get to pick which toppings we wanted for each of our pizzas. This pizza is a thick crust Sicilian style, so the pieces are very hearty, which meant we would have leftovers for the entire week!

Sauce Ingredients:
3 29 oz cans of crushed San Marzano tomatoes, in puree
6 cloves of garlic
3-4 filets of Italian brown anchovies
Sugar –1.5 Tablespoon per can (or to taste)
1 T sea salt
1 T oregano
1 T onion powder
1 T crushed red pepper
1 T black pepper)
3 bay leaves
1 T parsley
1 T basil

Sauce Instructions:
In a large 8 quart pot, pour olive oil in and sauté garlic and anchovies briefly. Pour in cans of crushed tomatoes. Add 1 C of water for meat sauce; ½ C of water for marinara. Add spices and sugar to taste. Bring to boil, then simmer for 1 hour.
Add meatballs after sauce has been simmering for 1 hour. Then, simmer for another ½ hour

Meatball Ingredients:
1.5 lbs. organic bison meat
4 eggs (substitute: pure olive oil, amount is a guess based on texture, which should be pasty)
1-2 T Italian seasoning
1-2 T garlic powder
1-2 T onion powder
1-2 T salt
1-2 T black pepper
1½ C almond flour

1/5 C coconut flour (substitute: reduce almond flour to 1 C, add 1 C Italian style gluten-free bread crumbs)
(Optional) Red wine, as much as you'd like

Meatball Instructions:
Place all ingredients into a large bowl and mix well until texture is pasty. Roll into tight golf-ball sized meatballs – makes about 30 meatballs.

In a large sauté or fryer pan, fill bottom with approximately ½ inch olive oil on medium heat. When oil is hot, add meatballs and cook about 5 or 6 minutes—then turn over gently with tongs. Cook another 5 or 6 minutes until slightly pink inside. Sear ends by standing on edges for a brief time

Add to sauce, simmer for 20 minutes

Pizza Dough Ingredients:
4 eggs
½ T sea salt
1 t garlic powder
1.5 T of ghee
¼ C olive oil
½ C warm water
1.5 T double acting baking powder
5 C almond flour
3.5 C tapioca flour
½ C coconut flour

Dough Instructions:
In a large stand mixer or by hand add eggs, sea salt, garlic powder, ghee, and olive oil and mix well. Then add water and double acting baking powder and mix well again.

In a bowl mix the almond flour, tapioca flour and coconut flour. Then slowly add flour mixture to the wet ingredients until all flour has been added. Continue to mix until it starts to form a dough. You can slowly add more water or flour until the texture is right. Since this is not gluten dough, it may not form well in the mixer without help. You may need to take it out and mix it in the bowl by hand until it forms, then put it back with the mixer.

Once the texture is doughy, take it out of the mixer and knead it well by hand on a wooden cutting board. You can break it into two or three separate balls to knead and store. The dough must be well mixed and not a grainy texture. It should feel like playdough and pull apart well.

Once it's done, wrap it loosely in plastic wrap and set aside for 15-20 minutes or so while you prepare the toppings. Since it won't rise, it doesn't matter how long it sits but wrapping it will keep it moist.

Pizza Toppings:
3-mild Italian sausages - cooked
4-5 cups baby spinach - cooked

mushrooms, sliced

two Roma tomatoes, sliced

3 cloves of fresh garlic, sliced

Pizza Assembly:

In a large baking pan with sides – 12 x 16, grease slightly with olive oil. Press pizza dough into pan until it's spread across entire pan. Use your palms and fingertips to get it even so it will cook well. Add marinara or meat sauce to top the pizza dough and spread evenly, cover well. Add all your toppings. Separate spinach leaves and spread across top of sauce. Sprinkle on garlic clove. Slice sausage into small pieces and spread across pizza.

Make half of the pizza for your family members who won't eat it without cheese (use two pans or share one, but note that cheese might melt onto your half). Add mozzarella cheese right after sauce, before toppings. Add meatballs to the pizza instead of sausage or add both. Add butternut squash. Get creative with other toppings. Drizzle olive oil on top of pizza and corners of pan.

Bake at 400 degrees for 40-50 minutes (or 425, depending on your oven temperature).

Cut off a corner to check if dough is fully cooked. If not, put it back in the oven until middle of dough is cooked and bottom is crispy.

Toppings Variations for the Rest of the Family

Dairy-free. Goat cheese or regular mozzarella cheese, butternut squash instead of cheese, pepperoni, Bison meatballs, artichokes, black olives

Sher's Gluten Free and Low Lactose Mac and Cheese
Sher Dulany

Growing up, macaroni and cheese was my favorite food. As I got older, not much changed. I still loved the taste of it and the simplicity of the meal. Adapting my meals to be low in lactose and gluten free was an adjustment, and one of the first things I had to modify was mac and cheese. This combination of ingredients is what works for me, but you could easily change the types of cheese to suit your taste better; Caylen likes his with pepper jack and medium cheddar. I have found that a whisk will work best to mix the roux with the milk, but make sure you use a silicone whisk so you don't disrupt the coating on your pot. I prefer using shell pasta because it acts like a little bowl to hold the cheese sauce, but you can use whatever you have on hand. This is typically a main dish in my house, but could easily be a side dish if serving more people. Enjoy!

Ingredients

2 T gluten free flour
1-2 T of ghee
Dash of Cayenne pepper
3 t sea salt
Ground black pepper
Tony's Cajun seasoning
2 to 2 ½ C Fairlife lactose free milk
1½ C shredded sharp cheddar cheese. Freshly shredded works best but frozen will work too
½ C shredded parmesan cheese. Again, freshly shredded if available
Gluten free shell pasta

Instructions

On one burner, bring water salted with sea salt to a boil.

On another burner, melt ghee into pot. Begin with one tablespoon. Once ghee is melted, add flour and mix well. The roux should be smooth and not lumpy; add the other tablespoon of ghee if needed. Mix the Cayenne pepper, black pepper and Tony's Cajun seasoning at this stage.

Slowly add ½ C milk and mix continuously until thickened. Continue adding the milk in this fashion until all of the milk has made its way into the pot.

Your water should be boiling at this point – add the pasta

Sprinkle in most of your parmesan and mix by gently folding in cheese. Using a small silicone spatula (think of something you would use for brownie mix) works well at this point. The remaining cheese will be used as a topping.

Once the parm is mixed in, begin adding the cheddar. Use small handful at a time and wait until it has been fully incorporated with the sauce to add more

Remove shells from boiling water once they are al dente. Pour some of the boiling water into the sauce. You only need a splash.

Dip a metal spoon into the cheese sauce; it should coat the back of the spoon. Take this opportunity to sample and adjust seasoning as needed.

Return shells to their pot and pour the cheese sauce over the noodles. Gently mix with the silicone spatula as the noodles are somewhat fragile, especially if you are using rice pasta.

Serve in a deep bowl and garnish with parmesan.

M'Jedra "Lentils and Rice with Salad and Yogurt"
Farah Family Recipe

M'Jedra is a classic dish in the Middle East, specifically Lebanon. Every family has eaten M'Jedra and it's a staple in almost every home. M'Jedra, in short, translates to "the poor man's dish" as all the ingredients are inexpensive and easy to obtain in a country such as Lebanon that often lacks resources. The following recipe reflects the way my family made it while I was growing up; my father is from the Northern part of Lebanon, an area called Akkar. If you're from Tripoli or Beirut or even the mountain region, the recipe might vary slightly. As a second generation Lebanese, I don't make it nearly as perfectly and delicious as my father does, but everyone seems to love it any way. Makes enough for 4 people. Time to Make: 1 hour

Ingredients
Lentils and Rice:
    1/8 C extra virgin olive oil
    1 small onion chopped
    1 C rice
    ½ C dried lentils (I used dried brown lentils)
    Salt – one tablespoon in the while lentils are boiling
Salad – all finely chopped
    Romaine lettuce
    Tomatoes (I use 2)
    English cucumber
    Radish (I use 3)
    Fresh jalapeños (I use ½)
    Use the vegetables to your taste.
Dressing – This is the ONLY salad I over-dress. It really needs to be nearly soaking in the dressing. Trust me. Adjust the amounts based on taste. Some people like more lemon, some less. You'll find what you like.
    2 garlic cloves crushed (more if you like it garlicy)
    1/8 - C fresh lemon juice
    ¼ -C EVOO
    Salt to taste
Yogurt
    3 C of plain, unflavored yogurt (regular or Greek depending on taste)
    ½ English cucumber, peeled and finely chopped
    2 cloves crushed garlic
    Dried and fresh mint to taste
    Salt to taste

Directions:

Soak the rice in water while you cook the onions and lentils. Wash the lentils (pull out any rocks), cover with water in small pan and plenty of salt, boil until just shy of al dente (do NOT overcook).

Heat olive oil in a medium sized pan; brown the onion. Once onions and lentils are done, combine the raw washed rice, par-cooked lentils with the onions. Cover with about ½ inch of water. Cook until rice is cooked! (You might need to add more water along the way.)

While lentils and rice are cooking, cut up the veggies and assemble the salad and the yogurt. Just before serving, dress the salad. Remember, the wetter the better

To serve, dish out lentils and rice, and then top with wet salad and/or yogurt to your liking

Indian Chickpea Curry
Kari White

This is a very flavorful vegetarian dish that is easy enough to make on a weeknight. You can also add roasted cubed sweet potatoes for a little variation.

Ingredients

3 T vegetable oil
½ onion, thinly sliced
¼ C raisins (optional) –it is nice and adds a little sweetness
6 garlic cloves*
1 inch ginger (peeled)*
½ jalapeño*

If you have a small food processor, put the chopped garlic ginger, and jalapeño in it with a few tablespoons of water and puree it. If you don't have a food processor, grate and chop garlic, ginger, and jalapeño.

1 T ground coriander
1 T ground cumin
¼ t cayenne
¼ t turmeric
1 t chili powder
¼ t nutmeg
1 to 1 ½ cup tomatoes – I used canned, but you can use fresh peeled
1 t salt
3 cans chickpeas—drained
6 T cream
4 T low fat/non-fat plain yogurt
2 t garam masala
1 t ground dry fenugreek leaves (optional)
¼ C sliced almonds (optional)

Instructions

Heat vegetable oil over medium high heat and cook onions until golden brown. Add raisins until they puff up. Add coriander, cumin, cayenne, turmeric, chili powder, and nutmeg—stir until coated. Add garlic, ginger, and jalapeno—stir for 30 seconds. Add tomatoes and reduce heat—cook two to three minutes until the tomatoes start to break apart. Add salt—stir.

Turn off heat. I do this to speed up the cooking process as you don't want to add yogurt to something too hot or it will separate. Add the cream Add the chickpeas

It if isn't too hot, add the yogurt. If it is still very hot, let it cool or add a couple of tablespoons of water. Slowly bring the chickpeas and sauce to a simmer. Doing this slowly will prevent the yogurt from separating. Cook until sauce is thick and clings to the chickpeas. You can turn up the heat to boil the sauce down.

Turn off the heat and add the garam masala.

Crush the fenugreek leaves (optional) into a power using your hands/fingers, add and stir.

Add the sliced almonds, stir and serve.

Baba Zinaich's Beans with Ham and Sauerkraut
Cheryl L. Ilov

Beans with ham and sauerkraut is the ultimate Eastern European comfort food. My maternal grandparents were from Yugoslavia, and mother and her siblings grew up eating this dish, which in Serbian is called Gra E Kupus. Every well stocked Serbian kitchen had the ingredients in the pantry or refrigerator. My grandparents even made their own sauerkraut, with my mother and my uncle helping by stomping the shredded cabbage with their bare feet.

My Baba often made this recipe for me and my sisters when we were growing up, and once we knew that the sauerkraut came from a jar instead of bare feet, we could't get enogh of it. Of course, my mother frequently made it as well, and even served it to company on occasion, which horrified my grandmother. Gra E Kupos was considered casual, peasant food, like the American version of baloney sandwiches. But my mother didn't care, and her company always raved over it.

I have never made this recipe for company, but I do make it for myself and my husband. When I do, the fragrant smell of Gra E Kupos still takes me back to my baba's kitchen, and the sweet, loving, kind-hearted, and gentle woman who loved us all so much.

Ingredients
1 small meaty ham bone
1 32 oz. jar sauerkraut
1 can pinto beans
1 medium onion, chopped
3 cloves crushed garlic
Pepper to taste
4 T butter
3 T flour

Instructions
Drain and rinse beans, then place in a crockpot. Add the ham bone, then cover with water just over the level of the ham bone and beans. Add onions, garlic, and pepper to taste, cover and cook over low setting for 4 hours.

Add sauerkraut, including the liquid to the crockpot. Remove the meat off the bone and return both to the crockpot. Cook on low for another 4 hours.

Melt the butter in a small saucepan, whisking the flour in the butter until it is a smoother consistency. Add to crockpot and stir well. Cover and cook or another 30 minutes.

NOTE: The original recipe calls for dry pinto beans, but even after soaking them and cooking them all day, they never became soft enough for my taste, so I improvised. I'm sure my long-gone Serbian ancestors would find it in their hearts to forgive me. Gra E Kupus is better the longer it cooks and is even tastier the next day. And the one after that. It also freezes well, so you can put leftovers in the freezer, if you have any. In our house the pot was empty after two days because it was so good. And, because there were so many of us.

Baba Ilov's Stuffed Cabbage
Cheryl L. Ilov

My father was twelve years old when he and my grandmother left Czechoslovakia in December of 1939. My grandfather was already in the United States, having gone a few years earlier to work in the steel mills of Western Pennsylvania.

My grandmother was a larger than life woman with a boisterous personality and boundless energy. She was also an amazing cook. When my family went to our grandparents' house, often the smell of Baba's stuffed cabbage (called halupki in Slovak), greeted us before she did.

Nothing pleased Baba more than watching her granddaughters enjoy her halupki, and she would encourage us to eat "just one more." Especially me, who she always thought was way too skinny by Eastern European peasant standards.

When you make her halupki, you won't have to encourage anyone to have just one more because they are just so good that no one can resist them. My Baba would like that and it would make her very happy.

Ingredients
1 medium head green cabbage
1 pound ground beef
½ C uncooked white rice
1 medium onion, chopped
1 T butter
1 T salt
1 t black pepper
1 pound kielbasa
1 16 oz. jar sauerkraut
1 large can tomato juice

Instructions
Cut four deep cuts along the core of the cabbage and place cabbage in a large pot of boiling water. Lower the heat but keep the water at a slow boil. Use tongs to remove the cabbage leaves as they fall away from the cabbage, carefully laying them over and upturned to maintain their shape and keep them from sticking together.

Melt the butter in a small skillet and sauté the onions until slightly translucent. In a large bowl, combine the onions, ground beef, salt, and pepper. Mix well. Carefully remove the large leaf vein from the center of the cabbage leaf with a sharp knife. Place a small amount of the meat mixture at the bottom and the center of the leaf. Roll up the cabbage and tuck in the ends. Continue until the meat mixture is gone.

In a large pot or Dutch oven, line the bottom with sauerkraut and juice. Top with sliced kielbasa and leftover cooked cabbage. Cover with tomato juice so that all the cabbage rolls are covered. Cook on medium low heat for 3 hours.

NOTE: I prefer using a crockpot instead and cook the halupki on low for 8 hours. Halupki is another one of those dishes that are even better the following day.

Tomato Sandwich
Cathy Miller

My mother always made the best sandwiches. She made this sandwich in the summer with fresh out of the garden tomatoes. When I asked my mother why her sandwiches were always so good, she said "It's all about the bread!" She used toasted wheat bread.

Ingredients
Tomatoes
Mayonnaise
Onion
Swiss cheese
Salt
Pepper
Wheat bread

Instructions
Toast your wheat bread either in the toaster or the oven until golden and crispy. Spread mayonnaise on each slice of bread. Assemble the sandwich with cheese and onion. Place the tomatoes on last and sprinkle with salt and pepper. Place the top slice of bread on and enjoy!

Satisfying Soups, Salads, and Side Dishes

"Unquiet meals make ill digestions"
Comedy of Errors, Act 5, Scene 1
William Shakespeare

Denise's Rustic Mushroom Soup

Marisa's Fried Spinach

Grandmother's Chunky Vegetable Soup
Darryl W. Thompson

My grandmother had 9 kids – 6 boys and 3 girls. The soup was a way of making sure everyone could eat.

Ingredients

1 lb top round steak cut into 1 inch thick pieces
1 large onion, chopped
3 carrots, chopped into small pieces
3 garlic cloves, minced
1 slice thick-cut bacon, chopped
1 (14 ½ 0z) can diced tomatoes
½ C long grain white rice
4 C small broccoli florets
5½ t freshly ground pepper added to pot

Instructions

Mix all ingredients well and cook on low for three hours in a crockpot or Dutch Oven.
Serve with Texas Toast.

Crockpot Potato Soup
Marilyn Ferguson

The morning my mother passed away in the Monarch from a brain tumor, Sharon, a nurse, was cooking this soup. Before we packed up Mom's belongings and left for home, we sat together and ate a bowl of this soup. From that time on, this soup has been a comfort for me and my sisters.

Ingredients
1 26-30 oz bag of hash browns
2 14 oz cans of chicken broth
1 10¾ oz can cream of chicken soup
¼ onion, chopped
½ t pepper
1 8 oz pkg. cream cheese
1 C milk

Instructions
Add first 5 ingredients to crockpot.
Cook on high for 1 hour. Stir and then turn to low for 2 hours.
Add cream cheese and cook until cheese can be stirred into mixture.
Add milk and cook another 30 minutes.

Tex-Mex Potato Soup
Sally Clark

This is a family favorite and cooked often. I adjust this as to the ingredients I might or might not have. I also add black pepper and salt.

Ingredients
3 large potatoes, peeled and cubed
1 medium onion, finely chopped
1 medium sweet green pepper, seeded and chopped
1 medium sweet red pepper, seeded and chopped
1 medium sweet yellow pepper, seeded and chopped
2-3 T butter
4 oz. cubed, cooked ham
1 T hot green chiles, chopped
¼ t white pepper
1/8 to ¼ t cayenne pepper
1 can (13 oz) chicken broth
1 egg yolk, slightly beaten
¼ C heavy cream (I use evaporated milk)
½ C shredded sharp cheddar cheese

Instructions
Cook potatoes in boiling water until tender. Drain. Reserve water.
Sauté onion and peppers in margarine until soft. Add ham, chilies, and seasonings. Cook 1 minute.
Combine potatoes and broth (can be put through blender). Add sautéed vegetables.
Heat soup to just boiling. Beat egg yolk with cream and stir into hot soup. Stir Well.
Garnish soup with cheese.
Enjoy!

Mom's Potato Soup
With a Few Tweaks From Her Daughter
Virginia K. White

I didn't ever pay much attention to the way Mom made potato soup while I was growing up, but one time when my husband and I had lunch at Mom's she served it. Warren loves potatoes and thought it would be a good idea for me to get the recipe. Mom, like many who learned to cook, did it by trial and error or by memory. So, Mom wrote out the recipe and at the end said, "I prefer not to autograph this recipe because it is the first time I have stopped to think of how much of anything I use." I loved that. So, I use her recipe and added a few ideas of my own.

Ingredients
3-4 medium sized potatoes
1/4 medium onion, chopped
3 C milk
2 T butter
2 T flour
Optional add ins: diced ham and bacon

Instructions
Peel, dice, and cook the potatoes and the onion. If you are using left-over ham, dice it and cook it with the potatoes and onion. Drain the potato water off and then add about 3 cups of milk. If you are using bacon, it should be fried crisp and added after the milk has been added. When the milk has reached the near boiling point, but NOT BOILING, set it off the burner. Cream together the soft butter with flour. Gradually add the butter and flour mixture to the soup. The soup should be creamy and fairly thick.

Add Salt and pepper to taste.

Note: I chop about three stalks of celery and add that to the potatoes and onion mixture before cooking. I usually add another cup of milk and adjust the butter and flour mixture so we will have some leftovers.

Kristin's Comfort Chicken Soup
Kristin Dulany

I made this up when we were snowed in one time. It's not only yum on cold, snowy, or rainy days, but it is one of my son's favorite comfort foods.

Ingredients
1 family size can of cream of chicken soup
2 large cans of chicken
1 48 oz box of chicken broth
1 bag frozen carrots
2 bay leaves
Poultry seasoning, salt, and pepper to taste
½ C water
1 bag egg noodles

Instructions
Combine all of the ingredients except for the noodles together in a pot. Stir until mixed. Cook on medium high heat until carrots are tender. Add 1 bag of egg noodles. Stir until noodles are covered. Continue cooking on medium heat until noodles are tender. Serve with biscuits.

Green Bean Soup
Cheryl L. Ilov

At the end of every summer, once the weather began to cool off, my mother would break out her green bean soup recipe. Even though it signaled the end of summer and the beginning of the school year, green bean soup was a kind of consolation prize. At least we had a pot of delicious green bean soup to comfort us as we said goodbye to summer and headed back to school.

My mom often called it her "singing soup," because when we had it for dinner, there was no conversation, just the sound of humming as my dad, four sisters and I "mm-mm'd" our way through a bowl of soup. Every year, when green beans are in season, I simply cannot help myself. I grab a pound of beans, a few potatoes, and hum all the way home.

Ingredients:
2 pounds fresh green beans, sliced into bite sized pieces
3 medium potatoes, peeled and cubed
1 C sour cream
½ stick butter
1-2 T white vinegar (to taste)
3 T flour
½ C flour

Directions:
Place beans in a large pot and cover with water to a level of 3 inches above the beans and boil on high heat until beans are slightly soft. Add cubed potatoes and salt. When potatoes are soft, add butter to the soup, and lower heat to medium low.

Whisk together the flour and ½ cup water until smooth, and add to soup, mixing well, place the sour cream in a medium bowl, and add a small amount of soup, mixing together to thin the sour cream and to make a smooth consistency. Repeat this step, then add sour cream mixture to soup, stir well, cover and cook on low for another 30 minutes.

Ham and Bean Soup
Marilyn Ferguson

My husband loved ham and bean soup. This was the recipe I always used because it was my mother's. When I cook this soup and smell the pot simmering, I think of my mom and my husband, who are longer with us. Mom was a marvelous cook and I learned so much from her.

Ingredients

1 lb navy beans

1 ham bone and ham meat

2 t dried sage

2 stalks celery

1 carrot

1 potato

2 onions

2 cloves garlic

2 T chopped parsley

Salt and pepper to taste

Instructions

Soak beans overnight. (Rinse, add 6 cups water and cover and soak.)

Drain soaked beans, add 2 quarts fresh water, the ham bone (after cutting off most of the edible meat), sage, and generous amounts of pepper. Bring to a boil, reduce heat and simmer 2 ½ hours. Remove bone. Dice onion, carrot, and potato. Slice celery and mince garlic. Add veggies to soup along with 2 teaspoons of salt. Simmer until veggies are cooked. Add ham meat into soup. Add parsley and salt to taste.

Ham and Bean Soup
Anne White

I made this soup often when my mom moved in with us because she loved it. I made it with chicken broth because it seemed to taste better.

Ingredients
2 quarts chicken broth
5-6 cans Northern beans
4-6 cloves garlic, minced
1 med-large red onion, chopped
3-4 meaty smoked ham hocks

Instructions
Boil broth, garlic, onions, and hocks for two hours. Add beans, stir frequently for three hours. Right before serving, remove hocks, cut meat into bite size pieces. Toss fat and bones. Serve!

Christmas Eve Bean Soup
Dawn Vaughn

We were given this recipe in a house warming basket and after that, I've made this soup for Christmas Eve for years.

Ingredients
2 C dried bean assortment
1 can Rotel tomatoes
1 onion, chopped
1 clove of garlic, minced
1 pound ham, cut into bites
Optional: ½ C barley

Instructions
Wash beans and remove any stones. Soak beans in 9 cups of water for 8 hours. Add remaining ingredients and simmer until beans are tender. If you have an InstaPot, this can be made without soaking the beans. Follow the directions for cooking beans. It turns out great!

Oyster Stew
Marinell Neuhaus

My mother met my father at Virginia Beach when he was stationed there during World War II. As the story goes, they had never had oyster stew before, but they ordered it because it was the cheapest item on the menu. At first they didn't care for it, but grew to like it. We have enjoyed oyster stew every Christmas Eve since. I must say that it is not the inexpensive soup they enjoyed. I have found that oysters are expensive!

I make oyster stew in a crockpot.

Ingredients
1 gallon whole milk (or a little less)
½ C butter
2 pints oysters
1½ t salt
1 t Worcestershire sauce (You can adjust the salt and Worcestershire to your taste)
Sprinkle paprika on top of each bowl of soup

Instructions
In a crockpot heat milk on high for 1 ½ hours. In a saucepan, melt butter and add oysters with liquid. Simmer on low until edges of oysters curl. Add seasonings. Combine with the hot milk in crockpot and stir on low for 2-3 hours, stirring occasionally.

Denise's Rustic Mushroom Soup
Denise Popish

This soup came to be when I grew my own mushrooms! I had bought one of those home kits to attempt to cultivate mushrooms. I had no idea how successful I would be! With so many oyster mushrooms, I needed a recipe that would use them, but also showcase their buttery flavor. What better way to do that than with than soup. It is hardy and creamy and a real comfort food, especially in the fall and winter months.

Ingredients

1 stick of butter

2 cloves of garlic – minced (always fresh)

1 large onion or two small, don't skimp – chopped smallish

Experiment with a variety of mushrooms and as much as you would like. It depends on how you like your soup. We like a lot of plain button mushrooms but also oysters and cremini.

Fresh herbs: thyme, rosemary, oregano and sage. I chop the sage but the rest I put in whole

Broth – I use chicken for lunches, beef for dinner, or in the winter; it's heartier. And, use just enough to cover the mushrooms so it depends on your mushroom load

1 C red wine + 1 for you. I use Merlot or Pinot Noir

Wondra or cornstarch (Wondra is a miracle and makes it so much easier)

1 pint of heavy cream or half and half

Salt and pepper to taste

Instructions

In a large stockpot, melt butter. When it has almost completely melted, add garlic and stir. You want the butter to grab the flavor of the garlic. Add onion. Sweat down the onions with the butter and garlic. Add mushrooms, herbs, and mix.

Add broth and wine. Simmer for about an hour or until the onions are soft and no longer crunchy.

Start sprinkling Wondra on top and stirring to thicken until you have your desired thickness. Remember you are going to add cream last, so it will thin out just a bit.

Add your cream, stir and simmer for 2-5 minutes. Serve with warm, crusty bread.

White Chili
Chery Lockhart Ogden

This recipe has been a favorite for a long time. So long, in fact, that I don't recall where and when it was received.

Ingredients

1 T olive oil
1 lb boneless, skinless chicken breast, cubed
¼ C chopped onion
1 4 oz can chopped green chiles
1 19 oz can white kidney beans – undrained
1 t California Style Blend Garlic Powder
½-1 t ground cumin
½ t oregano leaves
½ t cilantro leaves
¼ t ground red pepper

Instructions

Heat oil in 3-quart saucepan, add chicken and cook 5 minutes, stirring often. Remove chicken, cover, and keep warm. Add onion to saucepan and cook 2 minutes. Stir in chicken broth, green chiles, and spices. Simmer 20 minutes. Add cooked chicken and beans and simmer 10 minutes. Garnish with shredded Monterey Jack cheese. Serves 4.

Note: If you can't find white kidney beans and the California Style Garlic Power, substitute white Northern beans and plain garlic powder.

Texas Tortilla Soup
Cheryl Ogden

This recipe came from a good friend and it has become one of our favorite soups for a cold day. Excellent.

Ingredients
1 T oil
Onion – chopped
Garlic cloves – minced
2 16 oz cans of tomatoes – can buy tomato wedges
1 can tomato soup
1 can chicken broth
1 can beef broth
1 can diced Rotel
2 C cooked chicken
1½ C water
1 t salt
1 t sugar
1 t Tabasco sauce
1 t Worcestershire sauce

Instructions
Cook chicken and set aside. Sauté onion and garlic in hot oil. Add remaining ingredients and chicken. Simmer, but do NOT boil, for 1 hour.

To serve: Put tortilla chips in bottom of soup bowl. Ladle soup over chips. Top soup with shredded cheddar cheese and chips.

Tortilla Soup
Cari Southerland

Every recipe for tortilla soup that I've ever looked at has corn in it. I'm not a fan! Instead of following those recipes, or buying some soup I was going to have to pick stuff out of, I mixed together things that I liked. It's super easy, and can sit and cook all day either on the stove or in the crockpot. When my daughter was little, she tried to eat around the "chunks" – so I threw it all in the blender so we had smooth soup! That's the way we make it all the time.

Ingredients
1 onion, diced
3 cloves garlic, minced
1 large can of green chilies
1 can jalapeños, or diced fresh jalapeños
1 14 oz can tomato sauce
1 can diced tomatoes with green chiles (I prefer fire roasted)
6 cups of chicken broth
2 lb of chicken breast
Salt and pepper to taste
Fried Tortilla strips, shredded cheese, diced avocado for serving

Instructions
Sprinkle salt and pepper on chicken breasts. Grill, broil, or sauté until outside is brown. It does not have to be cooked all the way through, as it will cook in the soup.
Combine all canned ingredients in a large Dutch oven or stock pot. Bring to a simmer.
In a separate sauté pan, cook onions and garlic until caramelized. Add to soup.
Simmer all ingredients together for 1 to 1 ½ hours so flavors come together.
Test for seasoning with salt and pepper before serving.

Variations – Pulled rotisserie chicken can be used instead of raw chicken.
Combine onions, garlic, jalapeños, green chiles, diced tomatoes in blender, and blend until smooth. This will remove all chunks from your soup except pieces of chicken – great if you have picky eaters!

Mom's Cheeseburger Soup
Bob Bitzer's Mom

This has been passed down from Grandma Bitzer. With 24 grandchildren, she always had a pot on the stove when the family was home for the holidays!

This is one of our favorites!

Ingredients

½ pound ground beef

¾ C minced onions

¾ C shredded carrots

¾ C diced celery

1 t dried basil

1 t parsley flakes

4 T butter (divided)

3 C chicken broth

4 C diced potatoes

¼ C flour

1½ C milk

¾ t salt

¼ t pepper

2 C cubed American cheese

Instructions

In 3 qt. saucepan, brown beef, drain, set aside. In same saucepan, saute onions, carrots, celery, basil, parsley in 1 T butter until veggies are tender--about 10 minutes. Add broth, potatoes, and beef. Bring to boil. Reduce heat and simmer 10-12 minutes until potatoes are tender. Meanwhile in skillet melt remaining 3 T butter. Add flour, cook, and stir until bubbly. Add to soup and bring to boil. Add cheese, milk, salt, and pepper. ENJOY!

Trinity Square Care Moroccan Tomato Soup
Kathi Emry Vontz

This is similar to soup served at the Grateful Break and Freak Beat Vegetarian restaurant in Lincoln, Nebraska. It is sort of a hippie-type place that is fun and serves great food. I liked the soup enough to search for something close to what was served in that restaurant.

Ingredients

2 T olive oil
1 chopped onion
5 cloves garlic, minced
1 can tomatoes
1 C peanut butter
1 t cumin
1 T Tabasco
2 T cayenne pepper
1 T chili powder
2 T white vinegar
1 t salt
1 t black pepper
1 T sugar
¼ C tomato paste
2 C water

Instructions

In a large pan, heat oil and sauté onion. Add garlic for the last minute of the sauté. Place tomatoes and liquid in a bowl and crush (I use a stick blender). Add to the onion/garlic mixture and reduce heat to very low. Add peanut butter and stir until combined. Add cumin, hot sauce, cayenne, chili powder, vinegar, salt, pepper, sugar, tomato paste, and water. Stir until well combined. Cover. Cook at a low heat, and simmer for 10-15 minutes, stirring frequently.

Olive Garden Pasta e Fagioli Copycat Recipe
Kathi Emry Vontz

This is my favorite restaurant. This is my favorite soup!

Ingredients
1 pound ground beef
1 small onion, diced (1 cup)
1 large carrot, julienned (1 cup)
3 stalks celery, chopped (1 cup)
2 14.5 oz cans diced tomatoes
1 15 oz can red kidney beans (with liquid)
1 15 oz can great northern beans (with liquid)
1 15 oz can tomato sauce
1 15 oz can V-8
1 T white vinegar
1½ t salt
1 t oregano
1 t basil
½ t pepper
½ t thyme
½ pound Ditalini pasta (1/2 package)

Instructions
Brown the beef in a large pan over medium heat, drain off the fat. Add onion, carrot, celery, and garlic. Sauté for 10 minutes. Add remaining ingredients, except pasta and simmer for 1 hour. About 50 minutes into simmering, cook the pasta in 1½-2 quarts of boiling water over high heat. Cook for 10 minutes or just until pasta is al dente. Add to the large pot of soup and simmer 5-10 minutes more. Serve with some grated parmesan cheese and breadsticks.

Polynesian Salad
Louise White

The first time I had this salad was when my mother-in-law, Louise White, made it for a family dinner. I was not only in love with the taste, but with the ease of making it. And, you can make it a day in advance which really helps with meal prep! It has become a family favorite and some members even have it for breakfast!

Ingredients
1 pt. sour cream
2 cans drained Mandarin oranges
1 large can chunk pineapple, drained
1 package slivered almonds
Most of one bag of colored marshmallows

Instructions
Mix all ingredients in a large bowl, cover, and refrigerate several hours or overnight. You can actually use this basic recipe and use different fruits depending on the season or the colors you think would add to the festivities. I have sometimes added apples and bananas. Cut up grapes work well too.

Mom's Cranberry Salad
Virginia K. White

Mom used to fix this every Thanksgiving and sometimes at Christmas. I'm not a huge fan of cranberries, but I love them in this salad. The salad was requested at additional family meals as well.

Ingredients
1 pound grapes quartered
2 pounds cranberries – put through the food processor
1 C chopped nuts
1 C cream, whipped
1 C sugar

Instructions
Combine ingredients and let stand overnight. Be sure to cover it.
Variation: To add a little color, you can also add colored marshmallows

Mother's Cranberry Salad
Gina Sheridan and Flo Francis

Thanksgiving dinner was often accompanied by canned cranberry sauce at our house. That came from my sister and me who thought it was much easier to open a can than to make this salad. Our mother, Louse Evans, had a different idea, though. She preferred to get the cranberries served for this meal through means of a salad, rather than a sauce or sugary relish. We grew to love it because the salad is quite tasty and people like the sweet and tart mixture. This is rather time consuming but well worth the effort. Seriously.

Ingredients

1½ bags of cranberries (about 3 cups of cranberries)
3 C sugar
3 packages raspberry Jell-O
3 C boiling water
1½ C chopped apple
1½ C chopped celery
1½ C chopped nuts (she always used pecans)
1 small can crushed pineapple, drained

Instructions

Rinse the cranberries and put them through the food processor to chop up the raw berry. Put the cranberries in a LARGE bowl and pour the sugar over them. Set aside.

Boil water and pour over the raspberry Jell-O in a large bowl. Just use the boiling water. Don't add anything else to the Jell-O. This gelatin should be very syrupy. Set aside.

Once you have those two big items sitting and waiting, you can start to chop your apple, celery, and nuts. Chop them so that they are bite-sized. This is a good time to drain the pineapple as well. The cranberries should be in the largest bowl. When all is ready, pour the gelatin over the sweetened cranberries. Mix well. Then add the rest of the ingredients.

Our mother always put the mixture in molds. Flo and I told Mother years ago that we didn't use a mold. We used BIG Pyrex dishes to hold this large mixture. She couldn't understand it, as she saw the mold as an elegant way to serve the salad. I never saw my mother have difficulty unmolding anything, but Flo and I never had good luck. It is much easier to cut this into squares and serve on a lettuce leaf. Such a good salad.

Now, when Mother made it and I was still at home, I groaned and moaned about having to help. There is so much chopping, but it is a wonderful way to get others involved in the food prep. The food processor can really help with this recipe.

Thanksgiving is always on a Thursday, and I always make this salad on Tuesday or Wednesday. It is so nice to have it in the refrigerator and ready for the big meal.

Cranberry Mold
Beth McCane

This dessert/side dish is something my mom made for Thanksgiving and Christmas. The "salad dressing" is referring to mayonnaise. One variation is to add crushed walnuts. The reason the word "mold" is in there is because she used one of those green Tupperware Jello molds to put it in and then freeze it. Recommend thawing for at least 20-30 minutes before serving.

Ingredients
2 3 oz packages of cream cheese
2 T salad dressing
2 T sugar
1 lb can whole cranberries
1 9 oz can crushed pineapple
1 C Cool Whip

Instructions
Mix all together, pour into the mold, and freeze.

Celery Salad
Cari Southerland

I love celery and this recipe is celery overload! It's fresh, light, and super easy to make. Salads are always popular at our house due to their raw nature. Everyone loves the crunch! The hardest part of this recipe is trying to find heads of celery with lots of leaves on.

Ingredients
1 bunch of celery leaves from 1-2 heads of celery—choose ones with many leaves still on
3 sliced celery stalks
1 T minced shallots, or red onion
½ C fresh shredded parmesan cheese
2 T Extra Virgin Olive Oil
2 T lemon juice
¼ t salt
¼ t pepper

Instructions
Combine celery leaves, celery slices, parmesan and shallots in a bowl. Mix oil, lemon juice, salt and pepper together and dress the salad!

Curry Noodle Salad
Beth McCane

This has become a family favorite for my family mostly due to the history behind it. We got it from our new South African neighbors after they brought it to the 4th of July cookout. The very special part is that they wanted to be included in the neighborhood 4th of July celebration. They had never heard of potato salad. They even showed up with red, white, and blue plastic bowls to serve it. This curry noodle salad is delicious warm or cold. It's good year around, not just for cookouts!

Ingredients
1¼ package of curly pasta
1 bell pepper, diced
1 onion, diced
Marinade:
  ½ C vegetable oil
  ½ C white vinegar
  1 C ketchup
  1 C sugar
  1 T curry powder
  Salt and pepper to taste

Instructions
Cook and drain pasta. Mix pasta, peppers, onions, and marinade together until pasta is well covered. Best if left overnight or for a few hours in the fridge. Mix regularly while in the fridge.

Larapin Potato Salad
Virginia K. White

When my mother-in-law went to Missouri to help take care of her father, I cooked often for my father-in-law. He did not care for mayonnaise or onions, but I really did not know that. Because I don't really care for mayonnaise or much onion either, I have always used Miracle Whip and minced onion in my potato salad. One night I decided to make a potato salad because my husband is very fond of it. When Doc took a few bites of it, he declared it to be "Larapin." That was one of his favorite expressions if something tasted great. If he wasn't fond of something, he would usually politely eat it and then when asked how he liked it, he would say, "Well, I probably wouldn't order it in a restaurant." He always made me smile and I was always happy that he decided my potato salad was Larapin.

Ingredients
6-medium sized potatoes, cooked and cubed
5-6 hardboiled eggs – cubed
Minced onion to taste
Salt and pepper to taste
Miracle Whip – enough to mix well so it isn't dry. Don't mix it all at once. Just add it so the consistency is smooth but not sloppy.

Instructions
Combine all of the ingredients except for the Miracle Whip. Add in Miracle Whip to desired consistency. Refrigerate a few hours before serving.

Potato Salad
Cheryl Lockhart Ogden

This is an old Lockhart family recipe that was passed down to Cheryl from her mother. Jon Ogden, her husband, declares it to be his favorite potato salad recipe.

Ingredients

8-10 boiled potatoes – peeled and cubed

8-10 hardboiled eggs –cubed

1/8 C onion – chopped (or onion to taste)

Dressing

2-C mayo or Miracle Whip

2-T sweet pickle juice

2-t mustard

Salt and pepper to taste

Instructions

Place first three ingredients in a large bowl. Add dressing and gently mix. Refrigerate several hours before serving.

Seasoned Egg Salad
Rosette Obedoza

My mother gave this recipe to me. I remember that it was her favorite, quick, and easy potluck side dish.

Ingredients

¾ C mayonnaise

1 t curry powder

½ t salt

1 can crushed pineapple (well drained)

6 eggs, hard boiled and cut into cubes

1 stalk celery, sliced

1 stalk green onion, sliced

2 T raisins

2 T roasted cashew nuts, coarsely chopped

Instructions

Combine the first three ingredients. Mix well. Add the drained, crushed pineapple and the remaining ingredients. Toss lightly until well mixed.

Julie's Macaroni Salad
Cheryl Lockhart Ogden

My oldest daughter, Julie, was a fanatic about macaroni. She loved it. This recipe is very similar to the macaroni salad sold by Valentino's Pizzeria in Lincoln, Nebraska. Julie loved Valentino's salad so much that we came up with this version.

Ingredients
2 C salad macaroni – cooked
1 1/3 C chopped celery
¼ C chopped onion
1 C cheddar cheese, grated
¼ C pickle relish
1½ C mayonnaise or Miracle Whip
2 t sweet pickle juice
3 T sugar
1 t salt
1 t mustard

Instructions
Combine the first four ingredients together in a bowl and set aside.

Mix the pickle relish, mayonnaise, sweet pickle juice, sugar, salt, and mustard together. Add the dressing to the noodle mixture and stir. Chill until ready to serve.

Broccoli-Raisin Slaw
Cheryl Lockhart Ogden

This recipe came from the Havelock Methodist Church Recipe book. This is one way Cheryl was able to get her husband, Jon, to eat broccoli.

Ingredients
3-4 heads of broccoli, chopped or cut into small pieces
½ C raisins
1 small red onion, chopped
1 pound bacon
1 C Miracle Whip
½ C sugar
2 t vinegar
¼ C sunflower seeds

Instructions
Cook bacon slices and crumble. Combine broccoli, raisins, onion, and bacon in a large bowl. Mix together the Miracle Whip, sugar, vinegar, and sunflower seeds and pour over broccoli mixture. Mix well.

Chinese Cabbage Slaw
Cheryl Lockhart Ogden

This is something different and one of the family's favorites. Our youngest daughter, Wendy, lived on Ramen Noodles and Ranch dressing while going to the University of Nebraska. This became one of her favorite recipes.

Dressing Ingredients

2 T sugar

3 T red wine vinegar

1 t salt

½ t pepper

Package powder from Ramen Noodles (chicken flavor)

3 T sesame oil

1/3 C vegetable oil

Salad Ingredients

1 8 oz prepared cabbage slaw mix

1 8 oz chopped green onions (optional)

2 T toasted sesame seeds

½ C toasted sliced almonds (toasted in oven)

Package Ramen noodles (broken up)

Instructions

Combine and mix well the salad dressing. Mix up the salad ingredients. Add dressing to salad shortly before serving.

Note: If you double this recipe, use 1/3 cup oil and 1/3 cup water rather than 2/3 cup oil. 2/3 cup oil makes it too oily. Cabbage slaw mix only comes in 16 oz packages in our area.

Scalloped Green Tomatoes
Katherine McIver

If you love fried green tomatoes as I do or just have extra green tomatoes on hand, this a wonderful way to cook them. It is very simple, tasty, and delicious. You can also use a mix of slightly ripened tomatoes with the green

Ingredients

4 large green tomatoes, cut into ½ inch pieces
1 small onion finely chopped
1 clove garlic, finely minced
1 t salt
½ t freshly ground black pepper
1 t dried thyme
¼ t freshly grated nutmeg
3 slices of bread (any kind), cut into ½ inch cubes
Olive oil to drizzle over the top

Instructions

Preheat oven to 375.

Put the tomatoes, onions, garlic, salt, pepper, thyme, nutmeg in a large bowl and mix well. Toast the bread and add to the tomato mixture and toss. Turn everything into an oiled 9 x 9 inch baking dish, drizzle olive oil and place a piece of parchment paper directly over the surface. Cover tightly with foil, and bake for 40 minutes. Remove cover and bake 10 minutes longer, basting if needed. Serve hot.

Southern Green Bean Bundles
Heidi White Finley

This recipe is something my mother-in-law makes and many of the Southerners have this on holidays. It has become a favorite in our family.

Ingredients
2 cans whole green beans
1 pkg. bacon, preferably thick cut
1 stick butter
1 t garlic powder
3 T Worcestershire sauce
½ C brown sugar
Toothpicks

Instructions
Preheat oven to 375. Drain green beans and fashion them in bundles with enough beans in each to wrap with ½ piece of bacon. As you go, secure each bundle's strip of bacon with a toothpick. Place each bundle in a buttered 9 x 13 baking dish.

Put a small pat of butter on top of each bundle. Then dust the bundles with garlic powder and brown sugar, and a dash of Worcestershire sauce on top.

Bake at 375, covered with foil for about 30 minutes. Check for doneness of bacon and that the sauce doesn't burn. If you like the bacon a little crispier or the beans a little more wilted, you can finish cooking for another 10 minutes uncovered.

Mother's Green Bean Casserole
Gina Sheridan

For as many Thanksgivings as I can remember, my mother made this casserole for the big day. It was also a choice to take to any kind of potluck or to families in the church who needed comfort food. Serve it hot and bubbly and you have a real treat. My sister, Flo Francis, and I remember Mother making it. Mother was a wonderful cook. My friends loved to come to my house to spend the night and have Mother's delicious biscuits for breakfast, and I always asked for this green bean casserole for company food. This recipe is one of those that everyone remembered as belonging to my mother. And, it was always easy to find all the ingredients and have them ready at a moment's notice. Notice there are no canned onion rings in this recipe. Mother didn't care for them so much.

Ingredients
2 cans green beans, drained
6 green onions, diced (tops and all)
4-5 stalks celery, diced
1 stick margarine
1 can cream of mushroom soup
1 medium jar pimento, diced
1 medium package silvered almonds
1 can sliced water chestnut
1 roll garlic cheese (see note)
Bread crumbs

Instructions
Assemble all ingredients in a baking dish. Bake at 350 for 30 minutes.

Note: Kraft no longer makes the rolls of cheese they once made. We have had to improvise to get the garlic cheese. Velveeta works. Flo and I melt 8 oz of Velveeta in a double boiler and add garlic powder to the melted cheese. Use an amount that is to your family's taste.

Family Sweet Potato Casserole
A must on holidays
Kathi Emry Vontz

I discovered this years ago and it has become a tradition for the holidays.

Ingredients
3 C cold mashed sweet potatoes (without added milk and butter)

½ C sugar

½ C milk

¼ C softened butter

3 eggs

1 t salt

1 t vanilla

Topping Ingredients
½ C brown sugar

½ C chopped pecans

¼ C flour

2 T butter

Instructions
Beat the sweet potatoes, sugar, milk, butter, eggs, salt, and vanilla in a large bowl until smooth. Pour into a greased 2 qt. baking dish. In a small bowl, combine all topping ingredients but butter, then cut the butter in until it crumbles. Sprinkle on top. Bake at 325 for 45-50 minutes.

Gluten Free Fried Spinach
Later called Christmas Candy
Marisa Jones

The original recipe from my grandmother and then my mother is made with Swiss Chard and is traditionally made for holiday dinners and is eaten as a snack throughout the day while preparing the main course. There hasn't been one holiday in my lifetime that I have not made this recipe! When my sons were little, they were at first skeptical to eat it. On the spur of the moment, my then husband referred to it as Christmas Candy. The boys took a chance and it turned out that they loved it. All the kids in the house that day ate the Christmas Candy and couldn't get enough of it! To this day, it's still a household favorite.

Prep time: 10 minutes, Cook time: 35 minutes

Ingredients
Spinach bunch
2 eggs
2 t baking powder
½ C cassava flour (or tapioca/almond flour mix)
Salt
Black pepper
Italian seasoning
Oregano
Garlic powder

Instructions
Mix eggs, baking powder and flour in a bowl. Mixture should be thick. Add seasonings.

Wash spinach and take very wet spinach and add to a skillet. Cook for about 2-5 minutes until steamed fully. Add spinach and some of the spinach juice to the egg mixture and mix well.

In a non-stick pan, add olive oil (about ½ inch deep). Heat oil. Grab a small bunch of spinach with tongs and place in oil. Push down on top of tongs to make flat. Add as many bunches as you can in the pan. When brown, flip over and cook the other side. Place on paper towels to drain the oil. Sprinkle parmesan or pecorino Romano cheese on top.

Original: Use Green Swiss Chard
For Swiss Chard, boil the leaves for 1 hour in water until soft. Boil the stems for 1½ hours in water until soft. Cook leaves the same as for the spinach.
Cook stems by adding to an egg and seasoning only mixture, add gluten-free bread crumbs and fry.

Beets in Raisin Pineapple Sauce
Elaine Michaud

This was one of my mother's recipes and we loved it because it was different and delicious. She would make this at Thanksgiving instead of sweet potatoes.

Ingredients
½ C brown sugar
2 T flour
¼ t salt
1/3 C vinegar
1 C water or beet juice
½ C raisins
1 9 oz. can crushed pineapple
1 can beets – drained
2 T butter

Instructions
Blend sugar, flour, and salt in saucepan. Stir in vinegar and liquid gradually. Add raisins, undrained pineapple, and butter. Cook over medium heat until thick, stirring constantly. Add beets to sauce and heat thoroughly.

The Fall Special
Jennifer Condreay

This term is used often in my household—still by both sons—Clark at 37 and Davis at 32. It happens right around the time when summer is definitely starting to fade and the air is crisp. When I text them with a dinner invite, they will undoubtedly say, "We are having the Fall Special, right?" I am charmed that my daughters-in-law and many girlfriends along the way have learned that in September, this is what is at my table. The "special" is really not so special and quite simple: Breaded Pork Chops, Wild Rice with Mushrooms, and . . .Stuffed Acorn Squash. I assume every home cook can get the pork chops and rice down, so I am submitting the squash recipe below.

Ingredients
2 acorn squash
½ stick butter
1 diced apple
2 T raisins
2 T brown sugar
1 t cinnamon
½ t nutmeg

Instructions
Cut squash in half and place cut-side down on a cookie sheet. DO NOT take out the seeds and innards! That will dry out the squash! Bake at 350 for 35 minutes.

Combine all the other ingredients in a bowl.

Take squash from oven and scoop out seeds. Stuff squash with apple raisin mixture. Cut bottoms of squash to make them stand steady in the pan. Roast another 15 minutes.

Mom's Thanksgiving Dressing
Virginia K. White

I have no idea where this recipe originated, but I know for as long as I can remember my mother and aunts always made this at Thanksgiving and Christmas if turkey was on the menu. It has become a favorite even with the new comers to the family. I have modified the recipe to fit my time restraints and taste.

Ingredients

1 loaf of dried white bread or a bag of dried, unseasoned bread cubes from the bakery
1 large can of chicken—save the drained broth (Mom cooked an entire chicken, boned it, and cut it up)
½ med onion, chopped (I sometimes use less because I have family members who are not fond of onion)
2 large potatoes cooked and cut into small pieces
1 T sage and poultry seasons (Mom's instructions "At least")
¼ pound butter
Potato water
Salt and Pepper to taste
5 eggs beaten

Instructions

Mix all ingredients in a large bowl. Use the potato water and chicken broth to make the mixture moist. Sometimes I have added additional chicken broth as needed. Place dressing in a 9 x 13 greased dish and dot with butter on the top before cooking.

Bake at 350 for 30-40 minutes.

Cheesy Browns
Virginia K. White

My family loves potatoes! I cooked frequently for my daughter's family when she and my son-in-law both worked on Saturday and we took care of the grandkids. I was always trying to find something that I could prepare ahead of time, so we could spend more time with the kids. My grandson, Garrett, actually renamed this recipe and it has become not only a favorite, but almost a standard with many family meals.

Ingredients
1 package (30 oz.) frozen shredded hash brown potatoes, thawed
2 cans (10-3/4 oz. each) condensed cream of potato soup, undiluted
2 C (16 oz.) sour cream
2 C (8 oz.) shredded cheddar cheese, divided
1 C grated Parmesan cheese

Directions
In a bowl, combine the potatoes, soup, sour cream, 1 ¾ C cheddar cheese and Parmesan cheese. Transfer to a greased 3 quart baking dish. Sprinkle with remaining cheddar cheese. Bake, uncovered at 350 for 40-45 minutes or until bubbly and cheese is melted. Let stand for 5 minutes before serving.

Dumplings
Even Hughes

This recipe is from my paternal Grandma Hughes. She got it from her German mom. The dumplings are dense, rather like a firm pillow, which might seem weird to think about eating. But, on a cold day, they are deliciously filling.

Ingredients
½ C flour
½ C cold water
¼ t salt
1 C boiling water
2 T butter
2 T cream
5 eggs
2½ C flour

Instructions
Mix together the flour, cold water, and salt into a paste. Add 1 C boiling water. Cook until it thickens. Add 2 T butter and 2 T cream. Allow mixture to cool before adding the eggs. Add the eggs, one at a time, beating thoroughly after each addition. Add 2½ C flour. Stir just enough to mix. Batter should be lumpy.

Drop by tablespoons into boiling broth. Cover and cook 15 minutes.

Remove dumplings with slotted spoon, drop them into a pot of chicken soup at the table.

Bountiful Breakfast and Breads

"'Tis an ill cook that cannot lick his own fingers"
Romeo and Juliet Act 4, Scene 2
William Shakespeare

Orange Bread

English Muffins

Denise Popish's Naan

Blueberry Mango Smoothie
Larry Greg

When I discovered I was a diabetic, I wanted to find something nutritious as well as workable for me. This is a favorite treat that was just what I needed.

Ingredients
1 C milk
1 5.3 oz yogurt
1 C frozen mango chunks
1 frozen blueberries
¼ t cinnamon

Instructions
Put all ingredients in a blender and blend until creamy.

Wholegrain Jam Squares
Virginia K. White

This recipe was given to me by one of my students. She brought me a sample and I liked it so much that I asked for the recipe. This is a great breakfast snack if you are on the run or one that goes well with yogurt. It's a nice "pick me up" if you need it later. I use whatever preserves I have on hand, but we are especially fond of raspberry.

Ingredients
2 C Quaker Oats, uncooked
1¾ C flour
1 C butter or margarine
1 C packed brown sugar
½ C chopped nuts
1 t cinnamon
¾ t salt
½ t soda
¾ C (or more) preserves

Instructions
Combine all ingredients except preserves in large bowl, beat on low until crumbly.
Reserve 2 cups of mixture. Press remaining mixture onto bottom of 13 x 9 inch greased baking pan.
Spread preserves evenly over the mixture (I sometimes warm them in the microwave to make it easier to spread).
Sprinkle with reserved mixture.
Bake in preheated 400 degree oven 25-30 minutes. Cool and cut into squares.

Breakfast Chile Egg Casserole – good any time!
Connie Hirz

My sister-in-law gave me this recipe over 20 years ago. I have shared it with many others. It is great for breakfast, brunch, and even dinner. The leftovers are great reheated in the microwave. If you use this for dinner, a tossed salad on the side is perfect.

Ingredients
10 eggs
1 lb. cottage cheese
1 lb. grated Monterey Jack cheese (4 cups)
½ C flour
1 t baking powder
½ t salt
½ stick butter - melted
1 t onion powder
2 cans (4 oz each) of chopped green chilies – mild or one mild, one hot

Instructions
Beat eggs until lemon colored. Add cottage cheese, Jack cheese, flour, baking powder, salt, melted butter, and onion powder. Blend well. Stir in chilies. Bake in a 9 x 13 Pyrex pan at 350 for 35 minutes or until center is firm. Let sit 10 minutes before cutting into squares.

Served with salsa and/or a dollop of sour cream.

Christmas Breakfast Casserole
Judy Kenna

I make this dish every year for Christmas morning. It can be made ahead of time and starts Christmas day off with a hardy meal.

Ingredients

2 lbs. breakfast sausage
2 bags diced frozen potatoes
1/2 onion, chopped
Butter
Salt
Pepper
18 eggs
1 lb. shredded cheddar cheese

Instructions

Brown the breakfast sausage and set aside.
Cook the potatoes with the onion in skillet with butter, salt, and pepper and set aside when done.
Scramble 18 eggs.
Combine all ingredients above with the cheese and place in a buttered casserole dish. Bake at 350 for 45 minutes to an hour. Serve as is or in flour tortillas with salsa and avocado.

Spinach Quiche
Rosette Obedoza

My father's only sister, my beloved Auntie Mila, who succumbed to breast cancer in 2013, gave this recipe to me. A smart, strong-willed, and generous woman, she serves as my role model to this day. The memories of her in the kitchen cooking, laughing, enjoying company, and hosting numerous parties in her house were my most treasured ones.

Ingredients
¾ qt. cottage cheese
3 eggs (beaten)
8 oz shredded cheddar cheese
3 T all-purpose flour
1 small package fresh baby spinach, chopped
1 uncooked pie shell
1 Roma tomato, sliced

Instructions
Preheat oven to 350. Beat eggs together, then mix the rest of the ingredients except the Roma tomato. Pour into pie shell. Bake for 1 hour. Remove and place sliced tomatoes on top as garnish and bake for another 10 minutes.

A Relic From the French Revolution Quiche Lorraine
Jennifer Condreay

My mother sponsored an After-Prom breakfast at our house in my senior year. It was astounding for many reasons, the biggest being my strict Southern Baptist mother let me stay out all night with my friends and their dates. When I sheepishly asked her if I could stay out, she said "Fine and shall I have a brunch for everyone the next morning?" I didn't want to lose that moment because she was clearly sleepwalking when she agreed to my night out, so I simply said, "Oh yes. . .we would all love that." She quickly went to work on the menu and came up with a dish that had just come out of the French Food Fascination Julia Child had so wisely planted into American kitchens. It was the 70s mind you. Ahem. . .it was 1970 truth be told-the year of my high school graduation. Quiche Lorraine! No one had ever heard of it before! (Twelve years later, Bruce Feirstein would introduce his book: *Real Men Don't Eat Quiche: A Guidebook to All That is Masculine.* Clearly, quiche had become mainstream by then.) When my group of bedraggled friends arrived that morning, the tables were set with fresh flowers, Lennox china, sterling silver, and pink linens. The menu: Quiche Lorraine, fresh fruit, and cinnamon rolls—a brunch I have repeated more than 200 times in the past 50 years. Quiches are on our table every Christmas morning and have been the mainstay for baby and wedding showers. I even made 18 of them for each of my Farewell to Friends Brunches after weekend weddings of both my sons.

Ingredients
1 pie crust (Making your own would be best, but the frozen grocery store ones will suffice.)
2½ C shredded Swiss cheese
1 large yellow onion (For a milder truly French touch, use 3 leeks, white part only)
4 strips of cooked and crumbled bacon OR 1 cup cubed ham
7 eggs
1 C heavy cream
½ t each salt and pepper
1 t nutmeg

Instructions
Sauté the onion in a little oil until it is limp. Whisk eggs with cream and spices. Layer the cheese, onion, and bacon until the shell is filled. Pour the egg mixture over the cheese. Bake for 40 minutes at 375

Uncle Oscar's Velvet Waffles
Virginia White

My mom lived with her sister and brother-in-law while she was pregnant with me and then for six weeks after I was born. Uncle Oscar was a bit of a Renaissance man and could improvise with the best of them. The story goes that he was going to fix waffles for us one morning and discovered there was no all-purpose flour. But, there was plenty of cake flour. So, he used the cake flour and added a bit of his own magic. Top these velvet treats with berries and whipped cream, or offer a variety of syrups, nuts, or preserves. YUM!

Ingredients
3 eggs
2 C cake flour
1 t salt
2 C milk
3 t baking powder
½ C margarine

Instructions
Separate eggs into whites and yolks.
Sift the dry ingredients together.
Beat egg yolks and add milk and melted margarine.
Add flour and beat until creamy.
Beat egg whites until they hold a peak. Using a whisk, fold them into the rest of the batter.
Pour ¾ to 2/3 C batter for every 2 waffles into a heated waffle iron.

A Tribute to An Autumn Breakfast Pumpkin Waffles
Jennifer Condreay

My Michigan roots are always stirred when the weather changes each September. Autumn is always a time of renewal (teachers will identify with that!) and reflection for me. I travel back to Michigan each fall because the crisp fall air mixed with colors of rust, orange, red, and gold all make me pause and reflect. I can stare at a row of trees that have changed and am still stunned at their beauty. And, I will admit, Pumpkin Spice anything makes me happy. I served a brunch a few years ago for friends who were visiting us at our Lake Michigan cottage. It was going to be a perfect day of hiking and touring the backwoods of the Leelanau Peninsula on Highway M22—always at the top of the list for "Most Beautiful Roads to Travel in Autumn" by *Travel* magazine. No, I am not going to footnote that; you will just have to believe me. Oh, and if you don't own one, get a waffle iron. Create a waffle bar at your next breakfast gathering. You can make the batter the night before and store it in the fridge. Have guests make their own and have a wide array of syrups, nuts, berries, and whipped cream on the buffet.

Ingredients
2½ C flour
1/3 C brown sugar
2¼ t baking powder
1 t baking soda
½ t salt
2 t cinnamon
1 t ginger
¼ t cloves
4 large eggs
1 C whole milk
1 C buttermilk
1 C canned solid pack pumpkin
¾ stick melted butter

Instructions
Combine all dry ingredients. Combine all wet ingredients. Slowly pour the wet into the dry. This can store in the fridge several hours or overnight. When ready to make, heat your waffle iron. Use enough batter to fill your waffle iron. Serve with pecans, maple syrup or sautéed apples for the ultimate autumn touch.

Baked French Toast
Kathi Emry Vontz

This recipe came from one of my mother's favorite cookbooks. It always reminds me of her. I have all of her handwritten recipe cards and several spiral notebooks filled with recipes she copied, some more than once, which I love because that reinforces how much she treasured them.

Ingredients

2 T butter
2 large baking apples, peeled, cored, and sliced
1 C firmly packed dark brown sugar
2 T dark corn syrup
1 t ground cinnamon
8-10 slices French or Italian bread – 1 inch thick
4 eggs beaten
1 C milk
1 t vanilla

Instructions

In large heavy skillet, melt butter over medium heat. Add apple slices and cook, stirring occasionally until tender. Add brown sugar, corn syrup, and cinnamon to apples. Stir until brown sugar dissolves. Pour apple mixture into sprayed 9 x 13 baking pan and spread to even layer. Arrange bread slices in one layer on top of apple mixture. With fork, beat eggs, milk, and vanilla extract until well mixed. Pour over bread slices. Cover and refrigerate overnight. Bake uncovered in a preheated oven at 375 for 30-35 minutes until mixture is firm and bread golden. Cool in pan for 5 minutes. Invert serving tray over French toast and carefully turn both over to unmold so apple is on top. Spoon any apples or syrup left on top.

The Burnett Family Doughnut Recipe
Darlene Burnett Spinar

I really don't know which of my Burnett relatives came up with this recipe. I am guessing it was probably my mother's mom. You can tell when you read the recipe that it is an old one. And, it isn't very healthy, so we haven't made it much recently. Mom came from a big family, so you can tell this was intended to serve the entire crew. I decided to include this because it is old, takes me back to some early memories growing up, and the doughnuts are very tasty!

Ingredients
8 C flour
8 level tsp. baking powder
1 level tsp. salt
2 C sugar
1 tsp. nutmeg
4 eggs separated and set aside (the whites will be beaten until stiff and added last)
4 T melted shortening
2 C milk
4 eggs yolks

Instructions
Mix the dry ingredients in a large bowl and set aside.

Mix the egg yolks, melted shortening, and milk together and then add to the dry ingredients.

Beat the egg whites until they are stiff and then fold them into the soft dough. This dough is soft and is handled better if allowed to set for 10-15 minutes.

Roll dough out on a pastry cloth sprinkled with a little flour until the dough is about ½ inch thick. Cut with doughnut cutter. You can remove the holes and fry the holes separately in the deep fat that you use for the doughnuts.

Fry doughnuts in deep shortening, turning when one side is brown. The second side will not take as long.

Glaze
1 lb powdered sugar
1 T sweet cream
1 t vanilla
Water or milk enough to make a very thin glaze.

Instructions for Glaze

Mix together all of the ingredients in a bowl adding water or milk until the glaze reaches the consistency that you desire. Using a fork, dip the doughnuts in the glaze over the bowl and then allow to set on waxed paper.

Alternative: If you don't have a doughnut cutter, we found that you can also make twists or small balls or dough, fry them, and then roll them in a cinnamon and sugar mix or powdered sugar.

A Grab from Ina Easy Mini Sticky Buns
Jennifer Condreay

Of my many cookbooks and hours of watching the Food Channel, Ina Garten clearly is my favorite cooking expert. Her relaxed, simple recipes resonate with me. She does not spend endless hours cooking or making a plate look like a work of art. She makes straightforward food with a short list of ingredients. And, I love that she is not svelte and flaunting her cleavage during her shows! This recipe is a bit of a variation of her. I took out some of the sugar and butter because these things ooze with goodness and calories. I also made them "mini" so people can indulge as they choose. Don't go buy Duffy rolls for a special occasion when these are so easy to make!

Ingredients
1 package Pepperidge Farm Puff pastry sheets
7 T softened butter
1 C brown sugar
¾ C chopped pecans
3 t cinnamon
1 C golden raisins

Instructions
Roll out thawed puff pastry on a floured counter. Combine 5 T softened butter and 1/3 C brown sugar. Divide and spread that mixture on both pastry sheets. Slice each roll into 10 equal pieces, trimming the edges for cleaner cuts. Combine 2 T softened butter, 2/3 C brown sugar, and the spices in a bowl. Put a dollop of that mixture at the bottom of 20 cupcake holders/tins. Sprinkle the nuts and then cinnamon on top of that mixture in each tin. Place each puff pastry piece over that mixture in each tin

Bake at 400 for 25 minutes. Take out of the oven and cool 5 minutes. Turn muffin tin upside down and release the rolls. DO NOT let them cool in the muffin tin or they will never release.

Easy-as-Pie Banana Bread
Shilah LaCoe

Fall is my favorite time of year. The air is crisp yet heady with warm treats. I don't bake often, but when I do, it's usually this easy banana bread! The smell of the flour mixing with the bananas reminds me of baking bread with my Nonna as a child. It also takes me back to living in downtown Charleston, watching the leaves change and drinking spiked hot chocolate with friends.

Ingredients
3 whole bananas—fresh or frozen (you can use 2)
1 egg
1 t baking soda
1½ C flour
¼ t salt
¾ C sugar
1 t vanilla extract
1/3 C melted butter

Instructions
Preheat oven to 350. Spray a 5 x 9 loaf pan with cooking spray.
Peel the bananas. Mash the bananas in a large mixing bowl.
Stir in the melted butter, egg, sugar, vanilla, baking soda, and salt. Stir well!
Add flour gradually and stir well.
Pour into baking pan. Bake for 1 hour. Let cool before removing from pan.

Optional: Add a handful of chopped nuts or chocolate chips when you add the flour. You can also drizzle Nutella over the top once you pour the mixture into the pan.

Best Ever Banana Bread
Dede Stockton

Moist and sweet! If you are making different loaf sizes, please make sure to test with a toothpick often. A small loaf pan will take much less time. I have tried many banana bread recipes over the years, but have never found anything as good as this one. I received the recipe from a friend decades ago and have never gone back. I save up old bananas in the freezer until I have enough to make several batches at a time as they get eaten so fast. I need to make sure that I make many loaves in different sizes.

Ingredients
2 cups flour (add 2 T for high altitude)
2 t cinnamon
2 t baking soda
1 t salt
Add:
3 eggs
¾ C oil
½ C nuts or raisins
1½ C sugar
2 C mashed bananas

Instructions
In a bowl whisk together the flour, cinnamon, baking soda, and salt. Mix in the remaining ingredients stirring until just incorporated. Divide evenly between 2 greased loaf pans.
Bake at 350 for 45 minutes.

Orange Tiffin Bread
Virginia K White

My mother-in-law gave this recipe to me shortly after Warren and I were married because Warren LOVES this bread. I always make it at Christmas, but it is great one to have with a cup of coffee, tea, or a glass of milk. It has a fresh taste that isn't too sweet. The orange flavor is refreshing, and this is super easy. I usually make it in small loaf pans, but it certainly works well for a regular sized loaf pan.

Ingredients
3 C sifted flour
4 t baking powder
¾ t salt
5 T soft butter or margarine
1 medium, unpeeled orange
1 C sugar
1 egg
1 C milk

Instructions
Sift together flour, salt, and baking powder. Cut an orange coarsely and remove the seeds. This is added to milk, egg, sugar, and butter in a blender. The well blended liquid is added to sifted flour mixture in bowl. Batter is stirred lightly and should be like muffin batter. Spray pans with Pam or Olive oil spray. Bake at 350 for an hour if you use a regular loaf pan. Slightly shorter time if you use smaller pans. Test with toothpick. Let set a short time before removing from pan and slicing.

Quick Coffee Cake
Kathi Emry Vontz

This coffee cake is a long-time go-to for company or to take to a coffee get together. The recipe came from a dear family friend and always brings back memories of her.

Ingredients
1 yellow cake mix
3 eggs
1 can cherry pie filling
1/3 C brown sugar
¼ C sugar
1 t cinnamon
1 C chopped nuts
2 T melted butter

Instructions
Mix the first three ingredients in a large bowl and pour into a lightly greased 9 x 13" pan. Mix the rest (topping ingredients) and sprinkle over the mixture in the pan. Bake at 350 for 35 minutes.

Grandma Cederdahl's Swedish Coffee Cake
Janet Grabenstein

This is a recipe everyone seemed to ask for. Grandma was always asked to submit recipes to various churches or other organizations that were making up cookbooks for fund raisers. This has been in a few cookbooks, so some people in Nebraska might be familiar with it. This was always included at our Christmas gatherings. When my grandfather's family came to the United States, my grandfather selected the name Cederdahl, which means Cedarvalley. When I think of this coffee cake, I picture the old country with cedar trees and people gathered around a fire place with a hot drink and this wonderful treat.

Ingredients
1 C flour
½ C margarine
1 T water
1-C water
½ -C margarine
1/8 – t almond flavoring
¾ C flour
3 eggs

Instructions
Preheat oven to 350. Mix 1 C of flour, ½ C margarine, and 1 T water. Divide the dough into two parts. It should look like pie crust. Pat this mixture out on a cookie sheet, in two strips—each measuring 3 inches wide and 12 inches long.

In a small sauce pan, mix 1 C of water, ½ C of margarine, and 1/8 t almond extract. Heat until the margarine melts, and then bring to boiling point. Remove from heat and add ¾ cup flour. Beat until smooth. Add eggs, one at a time, beating well after each addition. Drop this mixture on the 2 strips that are on the baking sheet, in a "ridge" like manner. Make 2 rows on each strip.

Bake 1 hour at 350. Frost when cool.

Frosting Ingredients
1 C powdered sugar
2 T margarine
Cream
Almond extract

Instructions

Add a little cream to make it spreadable and a little almond flavoring. Frost and sprinkle with a few chopped nuts.

Boston Bread
Alice Weeda

Every Saturday morning was baking day in our household of 12 children. Mom and whoever was home had to help with the week's baked goods. Usually that involved 10 dozen cookies, a layer cake, and at least one kind of coffee bread. These treats were part of our sack lunches that we carried to school. I especially remember Boston Bread because we used Diamond Walnut tins to make the round loaves. For years I kept 5 tins that Mom gave me as part of a wedding shower in 1967. Somewhere in our many moves, I discarded them for "real" loaf pans.

Ingredients

3-C raisins

5-C boiling water

1-C brown sugar

5-T shortening

3-T molasses

2-beaten eggs

5-C flour

4-t soda

1-C chopped walnuts

2-t salt

Instructions

Mix together the raisins, brown sugar, shortening, molasses and boiling water. Allow the mixture to cool. When it is cool, add in the eggs, flour, soda, walnuts, and salt. Divide into two loaves and place in greased tins. Bake 45 minutes at 350.

Denise's Naan (an Indian bread)
Denise Popish

Although I grew up in a very Italian home, the one thing my mom did teach me was a love of foods from all over the world. Learning how to properly make my own naan was inspired by the desire for bread that was healthy and versatile. We love this recipe so much that you can find it all of the time in our home. We use it as bread, pizza crusts (especially great for breakfast pizzas) and even with our Mexican food. It goes well with green chili.

Ingredients
1 C warm water
2 T honey
1 .25 oz package dry yeast (about 2 ¼ teaspoons)
3½ C all-purpose flour (or 2 cups white whole wheat flour + 1 ½ C all-purpose flour)
¼ C plain yogurt
2 t salt
½ t baking powder
1 egg
½ C butter
3 cloves garlic, minced
(Optional topping: chopped fresh cilantro, crushed garlic, extra salt)

Instructions
Stir together warm water and honey until the honey has dissolved.

Add the water mixture to the bowl of a stand mixer with the dough attachment, and sprinkle the yeast on top of the water. Give the yeast a quick stir to mix it in with the water. Then let it sit for 5-10 minutes until the yeast is foamy.

Turn the mixer onto low speed, add flour gradually, and yogurt, salt, baking powder, and egg. Increase speed to medium-low and continue mixing for 2-3 minutes or until the dough is smooth. (The dough will still be slightly sticky, but should form into a ball that pulls away from the side of the mixing bowl.)

Remove dough from the mixing bowl and use your hands to shape it into a ball. Grease the mixing bowl (or a separate bowl) with olive oil or cooking spray. Then place the dough ball back into the bowl and cover it with a damp towel. Place in a warm location. (I set mine by the sunny window.) Let it rise for 1 hour until the dough has nearly doubled in size.

Meanwhile, heat the butter in a small sauté pan over medium heat until melted. Add garlic and cook for 1-3 minutes until fragrant. Then remove butter from heat, strain out and discard the garlic, leaving the infused melted butter behind. Set aside.

Once the dough is ready, transfer it to a floured work surface. Then cut the dough into 8 separate pieces. Roll each into a ball with your hands, then place on the floured surface and use a rolling pin to roll out the dough into a large circle (or oval, or whatever shape it takes) until the dough is a little less than ¼ inch thick. Brush dough lightly with the garlic-infused butter on both sides.

Heat a large cast-iron skillet or heavy sauté pan over medium-high heat. Add a piece of the rolled-out dough to the pan and cook for 1 minute, or until the dough begins to bubble and the bottom turns lightly golden. Flip the dough and cook on the second side for 30-60 seconds, or until the bottom is golden. Then transfer the naan to a separate plate and cover with a towel. Repeat with the remaining dough until all of the naan pieces are cooked.

Keep the naan covered with the towel until ready to serve so that it does not dry out. Serve sprinkled with fresh cilantro if desired.

Mexican Corn Bread
Sally Clark given to Susanna Clark

This is an old classic of ours. It says corn bread, but it's more like a corn pudding. Sometimes I add a can of regular corn too. Sometimes I add jalapeños and I've substituted Greek plain yogurt for the oil for a healthier option. We always had lots of Mexican dishes in our house and this was a favorite.

Ingredients

1 can creamed corn (17 oz)
1 can chopped green chilies
1 C of corn meal
¼ C Crisco oil or vegetable oil
1 egg
1 C milk
¼ t baking soda
½ t salt
Grated cheese (cheddar or jack)

Instructions

Mix well into buttered dish. Top with grated cheese (cheddar or jack). Bake 1 hour at 350 or in a crockpot on low for 4 hours.

Zucchini Bread
Anne White

I baked breads often when the kids were little. I wanted them to have something nutritious and yet filling. These two seemed to do the trick.

Ingredients

3 eggs
2 C sugar
1 C oil
1 t vanilla
3 C flour
1 t soda
1 t salt
½ t baking powder
3 t cinnamon
2 C grated zucchini

Instructions

Mix eggs, sugar, oil, and vanilla. Add flour, soda, salt, baking powder, and cinnamon. Add zucchini. Divide batter evenly between two greased and floured loaf pans. Bake at 350 for one hour.

Pumpkin Bread
Anne White

Ingredients

4 C flour

3 C sugar

2 t soda

½ t salt

1 t cinnamon

1 t nutmeg

4 eggs, beaten

1 C oil

2 C pumpkin

2/3 C water

Instructions

Combine dry ingredients. Beat eggs, add oil, pumpkin, and water. Blend the two mixtures and pour into two loaf pans (1/2 C nuts may be added) Bake at 250 for 1½ hours.

Chocolate Chip Pumpkin Bread
Virginia K. White

I found this recipe years ago in a cooking magazine and have made it every fall. It is requested by my kids and grandkids. After I took some to my hairdresser, she requested it as well. We love it because it is so moist and the chocolate chips add an additional treat.

Ingredients

3 1/3 C all-purpose flour
3 C sugar
4 t pumpkin pie spice
2 t baking soda
1 t-salt
½ t baking powder
4 eggs
1 can (15 oz) solid-pack pumpkin
2/3 C water
2/3 C canola oil
2 C (12 oz) chocolate chips
1 C sliced almonds, toasted if desired
FYI—I LOVE cinnamon, so I am generous with it even though the recipe does not call for it.

Instructions

In a large bowl, combine the first six ingredients. In another bowl, combine the eggs, pumpkin, water, and oil. Stir into dry ingredients just until moistened. Stir in chocolate chips and almonds (if desired). Pour into two greased 9-in, x 5-in loaf pans. Bake at 350 for 70-75 minutes or until a toothpick inserted near the center comes out clean. Cool for 10 minutes before removing from pans to wire racks to cool completely. You can wrap in foil and freeze up to 3 months. I usually use small loaf pans because I like to give the bread as gifts. This makes about 6-8 small loaves. The small loaves will not take as long to cook so watch them closely.

English Muffins
Virginia K. White

When I was teaching at Lincoln East High School in Lincoln, Nebraska, one of the history teachers gave me this recipe. We were chatting in the lunch room about cooking and she mentioned that she had a good recipe for English Muffins. I asked her if she would share it and good to her word, she gave it to me the next day. The other day my daughter asked me for the recipe and when I pulled it out, I noticed that it was very used and stained in places. So, I typed it and sent it to her. It has been a favorite in our family since about 1973.

Ingredients
1 packet of yeast or 1 T yeast
1/4 C lukewarm water
1 C milk
2 T sugar
1 t salt
3 T butter
4 C flour (plus additional for kneading)
1 egg, slightly beaten

Instructions
Add one packet of yeast to lukewarm water and allow yeast to soften.
Scald milk. Add sugar, salt, and butter to the milk. Cool the mixture to lukewarm.
Add 2 C flour to the milk mixture and mix well. Add softened yeast and egg. Beat thoroughly
Add 2 more cups of flour to make moderately soft dough. Knead dough on floured board until smooth and satiny. Place in buttered bowl, cover with towel, let rise 1 hour or until doubled in size
Punch down the dough and then allow to rest 10 minutes.
Roll out until ¼ inch thick on lightly covered with corn meal board. Cut into 2 inch rounds. Cover with towel, rest 45 minutes.
Bake in ungreased, heavy skillet – hot at first, then reduce heat to brown slowly. I have best results in an electric skillet set at 340, but I have used a heavy skilled on the stove. Bake 10 minutes on each side. These toast best in a toaster oven.

Sweet Roll Dough – Sometimes Cinnamon Bread Dough
Virginia K. White

I actually have no idea where I got this recipe. I have always loved to bake bread and when we were living in Lincoln, Nebraska, someone gave this to me. I made white bread loaves with it and they were always a hit! Hot out of the oven with butter or toasted with butter and jam. One day I decided I might be able to make cinnamon rolls with the recipe and ended up making cinnamon bread. That has been a major hit for years and is frequently requested.

Ingredients
½ C warm water
2 pkg. active dry yeast
1½ C milk (lukewarm)
2 T salt
½ C soft butter
7-7½ C flour
½ C sugar
2 eggs

Instructions
In a bowl, dissolve yeast in water. Add milk, sugar, salt, egg, butter and ½ flour to yeast. Mix with spoon until smooth. Add enough remaining flour to handle easily. Turn onto lightly floured board, knead until smooth—about 5 min. Round up on greased bowl. Bring greased side up. Cover with cloth. Let rise in warm place until double— about 1½ hours. Punch down. Let rise again until almost double—about 30 minutes. Shape and let rise in pans and then bake 15-20 min. in 400 degree oven.

If you decide to make cinnamon bread, roll out dough in a circle, appropriate to the loaf pan size you are using. Spread soft butter all over the dough and then sprinkle with cinnamon and sugar. (I love plenty of cinnamon and sugar, so I am not skimpy with it.) Roll the dough up and fit it neatly in the loaf pan. I use the small loaf pans, but the standard size works well too.

Sweet Treats and Snacks

"When I'm in trouble, eating is the only thing that consoles me. Indeed, when I am in really great trouble, as anyone who knows me intimately will tell you, I refuse everything except food and drink."
Algernon Moncrieff, from *The Importance of Being Ernest (Act 2)*
Oscar Wilde

Denise's Fall Pumpkin Dump
Cake

Dede Stockton's Ice Cream Freezer

Cheryl Townsley's Caramel Corn

Cheryl Iloy's Grandmother's Reindeer
Cookies

Finished cookie trays

Judy Kenna's gathering to make holiday cookies

Grandma's Raisin Pie
Marilyn Ferguson

This is my grandma's recipe and we had this pie every Thanksgiving dinner. I learned to bake with Grandma and have the most wonderful memories of working beside her in her kitchen. She measured with a handful, a pinch, or a dash. She was my rock.

Ingredients

2 C raisins
2 C boiling water
½ C sugar
2 T flour
1/8 t salt
2 T lemon juice
1 T butter
1 pie crust

Instructions

Boil the raisins and water for five minutes.

Combine sugar, flour, and salt. Mix and add this to cooked raisins. Bring to a full boil. Cook one minute. Remove from heat and add lemon juice. Add butter. Pour into pie crust and bake at 375 until crust is golden brown.

Alice's Sour Cream Raisin Pie
Kathi Emry Vontz

Alice's pies in the long-ago popular restaurant in Lincoln, Nebraska, was a favorite place of mine to meet friends and family for breakfast. They served great home cooked meals and specialized pies. We often took home one of Alice's pies. This was one of my favorites.

Ingredients
1 C sour cream
½ C raisins
1¼ C sugar
½ t cinnamon
½ t cloves
Pinch of nutmeg
3 eggs, separated
2½ T cornstarch

Directions
Cook raisins in 1 cup water. Add 1 cup of sugar and spices and cornstarch to egg yolks with enough water to mix well. Add to raisin mixture and cook until thickened, then add 1 cup sour cream and cook only until well mixed and heated through. Pour into baked pie shell. Beat egg whites with ¼ cup sugar for meringue. Spread over filling and brown in a 350 degree oven for about 10 minutes.

Chess Pie
Janet Grabenstein

My grandmother, Dorothy Cederdahl, always made this pie for the winter holiday season. It was quite often one of many Thanksgiving pies, but it was always one we could count on at Christmas time. All in the family have the recipe, but it just never seems the same when we make it as when Grandma made it. Chess pie always makes me think of Christmas and my grandmother.

Ingredients
1 C raisins
2 eggs, separated
3/4 C sugar
3 T flour
1 pint milk
1/8 t salt
3 T butter
1/2 C walnuts
1 t vanilla
1 pie shell
2 T sugar
1/2 t vanilla

Instructions
Cook raisins in a cup of water, drain off juice and do not save the juice. To raisins add egg yolks and ¾ cup white sugar. Stir thoroughly and add flour, milk, and salt. Cook the mixture until it is thick, add butter and then add the walnuts. Bring to a boil for a few seconds, then remove from the heat and add 1 teaspoon vanilla. Pour into a pre-baked pie shell.

Make meringue with 2 egg whites. Beat egg whites until stiff and then add 2 tablespoons sugar, ½ teaspoon vanilla, and beat it well.

Spread over the top of pie filling and bake a few minutes until meringue is browned.

Let cool completely before serving.

Chocolate Pumpkin Pie
Jodi Bowersox

I was describing this special Thanksgiving pie in my novel, *Interiors By Design*: "She could see that the pie was anything but ordinary. Swirled with cream cheese and with a layer of chocolate on the bottom." I have no idea where that came from as I had never eaten a pie like that in my life. It sounded so yummy, though, that I went searching for a similar recipe. I found pumpkin pies with chocolate and pumpkin pies swirled with cream cheese, but not both. So, I put them together to create this delicious recipe.

Ingredients
1 unbaked 9" deep dish pie crust
1 C semi-sweet chocolate chips
3 oz. cream cheese, softened
½ C light corn syrup, divided
½ t vanilla
1 C pumpkin puree
½ C evaporated milk
2 large eggs
¼ C sugar
2 t pumpkin pie spice
¼ t salt

Instructions
Make pie crust. Sprinkle chocolate chips in an even layer over the crust.
Preheat oven to 325 degrees.
Beat cream cheese in a small bowl until light and fluffy. Gradually add 1/4 C corn syrup and vanilla; beat until smooth.
Combine pumpkin, evaporated milk, eggs, 1/4 C corn syrup, sugar, pumpkin pie spice and salt in medium bowl. Pour into pie shell.
Streak cream cheese across pie filling in stripes. Run knife down and up through the cream cheese. Bake 65 minutes or until knife inserted near the center comes out clean.

Chocolate Peanut Butter Pie
Kathi Emry Vontz

This pie is a favorite one from one of my best friends!

Ingredients
1¾ C crushed chocolate cookie crumbs (about 6 oz)
3 T brown sugar
5 T butter, melted
1 C creamy peanut butter
1 C powdered sugar
8 oz. cream cheese, softened to room temperature
1 t pure vanilla
1 C heavy whipping cream
Toppings optional: additional sweetened whip cream or crushed or chopped candy bar or nuts

Instructions
For the crust, preheat the oven to 375. In a medium bowl, toss the cookie crumbs together with the brown sugar. Stir in the melted butter and mix until well combined. Press the mixture evenly into the bottom and up the sides of a 9" pie plate. Bake for 8 minutes. Remove from oven and let cool completely.

For the pie filling, combine all the ingredients in a high-powered blender and mix until smooth and very thick. If you don't have a blender, use a large bowl of either an electric stand mixer or a hand-held electric mixer and beat the peanut butter, sugar, cream cheese and vanilla together until creamy. In another bowl, whip the cream to medium stiff peaks and fold gently into the peanut butter mixture until combined.

Spread the peanut butter filing into the cooled crust, cover lightly with plastic wrap and put in the refrigerator for 1-2 hours. Add a dollop of whipped cream or sprinkle chopped peanuts if desired.

Mom's Apple Pie
Alyssa C. Ilov

My mom learned how to make her famous crowd-pleasing apple pie from my grandmother. Our entire family loves it so much that every Thanksgiving my mom made both a pumpkin pie and an apple pie for us. What a woman.

After I left home and Thanksgiving rolled around, I craved my mom's apple pie. Since I had the recipe, I decided to forge ahead and give it a try. It was not an easy recipe and rather time consuming, but the results were worth it.

The pie tasted exactly like my mom's, and maybe even a little bit better, but I thought perhaps it was just my imagination. However, my dad confirmed my suspicions a few years later when I made it for him and my mom after I moved back to my hometown. My dad pulled me aside and told me that my apple pie was even better than my mom's, but he wouldn't dare tell her. It was our little secret.

From that time on, every time I served apple pie, my dad would look at me and give me a wink and a nod. When my mother wasn't looking, of course. To this day, when I bake my apple pie, I can still see my dad giving me his approval with a wink and a nod. That's when I know my pie is perfect.

Ingredients for Crust
2 C sifted all-purpose flour
1 t salt
2/3 C shortening
5-7 T cold water (you may need a few more)

Instructions for Crust
Sift flour and salt together; cut in shortening with a pastry blender until pieces are the size of small peas. (for extra tender pastry, cut in half the shortening until it is like corn meal. Cut in remaining until like it is small peas.) Sprinkle 1 T water over part of the mixture. Gently toss with a fork, then push to side of bowl. Repeat until all is moistened. Form into 2 balls. Flatten on lightly floured surface by pressing with edge of hand 3 times across in both directions. Roll from center to edge until 1/8 inch thick.

Ingredients for Pie Filling
6-8 tart green apples, pared, cored, and thinly sliced (about 6 cups)
¾-1 C sugar
2 T all-purpose flour
½-1 t ground cinnamon
Dash of nutmeg

Instructions

Pre-heat oven to 400

If apples lack tartness, sprinkle with about 1 T lemon juice. Combine sugar, flour, spices, and dash salt; mix with apples. Line 9" pie plate with pastry. Fill with apple mixture; dot with butter. Adjust top crust, cutting slits for escape of steam; seal. Sprinkle with sugar. Cover edges of pie crust with aluminum foil to prevent burning. Remove approximately 10 minutes before done. Bake at 400 for 50 minutes or until done.

Alice's Coconut Cream Pie
Kathi Emry Vontz

This is another delicious pie recipe from the long-ago popular restaurant in Lincoln, Nebraska. I have wonderful memories of spending time with family and friends at this restaurant. Their pies were always something you wanted to take home so you could enjoy a bit more.

Ingredients
2½ C milk, scalded
½ C milk
¾ C sugar
2½ T cornstarch
3 eggs, separated
½ C shredded or flaked coconut
1 pie shell

Instructions
Mix egg yolks, cornstarch, and sugar with ½ C milk and add to 2½ C scalded milk. Cook until thick. Add the coconut and pour filling into baked pie shell. Make the meringue for the top by beating egg whites with ¼ C sugar. Spread it over the filling and brown in the oven for about 10 minutes at 350. You can substitute banana or pineapple for the coconut.

Pepparkaka (Swedish Spice Cake)
Yael Abrahamsson

My dad was from Stockholm, and I have fond memories of him and my mom baking all sorts of things for parties. He made beautiful Princess Tortes (something I have never mastered, though I remember getting to help color the marzipan for the covering and decorations) and Swedish coffee bread and something he called Lillian Buns. This spice cake always made its appearance for dinner parties. It's super easy, and it always reminds me of my dad. This is the recipe he and my mother used.

Ingredients
4 C all-purpose flour
2 T baking soda
2½ C sugar
2 eggs
4 T butter
2 C buttermilk
2 t cinnamon
2 t cloves
2 t cardamom

Instructions
Preheat oven to 350. Grease Bundt pan with butter and coat with bread crumbs (I often just use Pam and then coat with bread crumbs).

Combine the melted butter, buttermilk, and eggs. Add in the dry ingredients and mix until batter is smooth and all lumps are gone.

Spoon into the Bundt pan. Bake 45-50 minutes, until tester comes out clean. Let the cake cool in the pan for 5-10 minutes, then remove to plate.

Notes: I like the way this bakes evenly in a Bundt pan. You can halve the recipe and bake it in loaf pans, and I've even done it as muffins.

Cocoa Spice Cake (Arabia)
Virginia K. White

I taught World Humanities for years. Students were to select a book to read outside of class, do research on the country and the author, and make a presentation to the class teaching them about the culture and the book. Most students decided to bring some kind of food that was typical of the culture or mentioned in the book. So, this recipe actually came from a former student. We all loved it so much that we asked for the recipe.

Ingredients
2 C flour
½ t salt
½ t cardamom
2 T cocoa
½ t nutmeg
1¼ C sugar
1 t baking powder
1 t cinnamon
1 t cloves
2 eggs
1 C milk
2/3 C shortening
¾ C orange juice

Instructions
Mix together first 10 ingredients. Add next 4 ingredients. Mix well by hand, incorporating as much air as possible. Pour into 2 greased and floured cake pans. Bake at 350 for 30-35 minutes or until cake tests done. Cool on wire rack.

Cocoa Frosting
2/3 pkg. powdered sugar
1/3 C shortening
2 T cocoa
1/3 C strong coffee

Instructions
Combine all ingredients until they are of spreading consistency. Frost cake. Top with nuts, coconut or powdered sugar.

Great Aunt Corie's Angel Food Cake Filling
Vyrla Jackson

My great aunt, Corie Burcham Hannencamp, lived most of her life in and around Hickman, Nebraska. She was the local telephone operator. She made her own angel food cake for this recipe, but you can use a box mix or a purchased angel food cake.

Ingredients
4 egg yolks, beaten well
¾ C sugar
1½ C milk
1 packet unflavored gelatin
2 T flour
1 C whipping cream
1 t almond extract

Instructions
Put gelatin in some of the milk and let stand. Combine other ingredients in a double boiler and cook until hot and thickened, stirring often. Add gelatin and stir until mixture is hot. Cool in a pan with the lid on.

Whip whipping cream and fold into the cooled gelatin mixture. Flavor with almond flavoring. Split angel food cake, fill and frost. Refrigerate.

Mom's Angel Food Cake
Virginia K. White

Mom made this recipe many times. When she had farm fresh eggs, we could expect this delicious angel food cake. With frosting or whipped cream and fresh strawberries, it was the best!

Ingredients
1½ C sugar
1 t cream of tartar
1 C cake flour
1½ C egg whites (about 12 eggs)
¼ t salt
1 t vanilla (almond if desired)

Instructions
Sift sugar and cream of tartar. Sift flour, measure, and sift again with ½ cup of the sugar. Beat egg whites on high speed until they hold soft but firm peaks. Add sugar and salt on low speed, then flavoring. Add the flour (sifted with ½ cup sugar) with wire whisk. Preheat oven and tube cake pan to 400. Put cake batter in hot pan and bake 22 minutes at 400. Turn upside down until cool.

Bailey's Irish Cream Cake
Margie Smith

Bailey's Irish Cream cake has always been our go-to cake for holidays, birthdays, and anniversaries. We love it!

Ingredients
1 yellow cake mix
1 3 oz. pkg. Instant vanilla Pudding
2 eggs
1¼ C milk
¼ C Bailey's Irish Cream
¼ t nutmeg

Instructions
Mix all ingredients together and pour into a prepared cake pan. Bake at 350 for 40-45 min.

Glaze
1½ C powdered sugar
2 T Bailey's Irish Cream
Dash of nutmeg
2 T milk

Instructions
Mix together all ingredients. Drizzle over the cooled cake.

Mom's Apple Cake with Caramel Sauce
Connie Hirz

My maternal great grandparents homesteaded in the Wheatland, Wyoming, area in 1895. My grandmother taught in a one room school house from 1903-1906. She rode a horse to the school every day. Married women were not allowed to teach, so once she married my grandfather, she had to resign. My maternal grandparents homesteaded outside of Riverton, Wyoming, when it was opened up for homesteading in 1915. My grandmother was a wonderful cook, but never measured anything. I'm not sure she owned a cookbook. There was always a pie sitting out ready to be eaten. My mother was also a wonderful cook and fortunately, she did measure and used recipes. This fall dessert recipe of hers has always been a hit when served to guests.

Ingredients
1 C sugar
¼ C butter
1 t baking soda
¼ t salt
½ t nutmeg
1½ t cinnamon
½ C nuts
1 t vanilla
1 C flour
2 large eggs
3 C chopped apples

Instructions
Mix all ingredients for cake. Bake at 300 for 60 minutes in a 9 x 9 greased pan.

Sauce:
½ C butter
1 cup half and half cream
½ C white sugar
½ C brown sugar
1 t vanilla

Instructions
Combine ingredients in a medium saucepan over medium heat until sugar is dissolved. Pour warm sauce over individual pieces of cake and serve immediately.

Apple Pudding Cake with Butterscotch Sauce
Patricia Winter

My aunt Isabel, my grandmother's eldest daughter and my favorite aunt, always had family dinners at her house when we visited Independence, Kansas. Isabel was a cheerful, loving woman who was always curious about new things. My favorite dessert that she made was Apple Pudding Cake with Butterscotch Sauce.

Ingredients

10 apples (about 6 cups) peeled and diced fine but not ground
2 C sugar
½ C Crisco
1 t salt
2 eggs
2½ C flour
1½ t soda
1 t nutmeg
1 t cinnamon
¼-½ C nuts

Instructions

Mix by regular cake method. Bake in sheet pan 9x12x3 or larger at 350 for about 45-60 minutes. Serve with whipped cream or butterscotch sauce.

Butterscotch Sauce:

2 C brown sugar
3 T flour or a little less cornstarch
1½ C boiling water
4 T butter
½ t vanilla.

Instructions

Combine all ingredients. Cook until thick. Pour over cooled cake.

Fall Pumpkin Dump Cake
Denise Popish

This cake came about when I was looking for a quick and easy dessert after a lighter meal. After looking through my pantry, I had all the ingredients for a dump cake but no canned fruit. Then I saw the canned pumpkin I had bought to make muffins. Good enough! Added the eggs to firm up the pumpkin and all my favorite fall spices and voila, Pumpkin Dump Cake was born! I'm sure it would be great with vanilla ice cream, but all we had was whipped cream, so that's what we topped it with. My family also commented that chocolate chips with the pecan might have been a good option.

Ingredients
30 oz. canned pumpkin
16 oz. sweetened condensed milk
1 t vanilla
1 t ginger
1 t apple pie spice
4 eggs beaten
2 t cinnamon
1 package yellow or white cake mix
1 C or more chopped pecans
1½ sticks of butter cut in pats

Instructions
Preheat oven to 350. Mix pumpkin, milk, spices, eggs, vanilla, and cinnamon in a large bowl. Pour into a greased and floured 9 x 13 pan. Sprinkle cake mix and chopped pecans on top. Cut butter very thin and cover all over cake mix.

Bake 1 hour and serve warm with whipped cream or vanilla ice cream.

Mrs. Remmert's Ultimate Chocolate Cake
Jennifer Condreay

I grew up in suburban Detroit, so "Farm Recipe" was never included in my cooking repertoire. If it were in one of the *Bon Appetits* that I have received monthly since 1977-yes. I still have all of them and still subscribe—then I would have pounced on a deeply rich chocolate cake recipe. But then I met my husband, Dennis in 1976, and I would soon adopt a chocolate cake recipe that stands up to any of the featured concoctions from any gourmet publication. Dennis's family were Colorado Homesteaders. Until I met them, I did not know what that term meant! They literally came to Colorado and staked a claim on land in Holyoke and started a legacy of wheat farming. His family's summer vacation was devoted to three weeks in August working the harvest. Dennis was 10 years old when he learned to drive the combine in those fields in Northern Colorado. The men would wake at 5 a.m. to go into the fields and the women would arrive at their posts in the kitchen to create the mid-day supper. Dennis fondly remembers those meals of fried chicken, potato salad, freshly made rolls, and iced tea. One summer an aunt brought lemonade and was touted as being too "uppity." The women would pack up the back of a station wagon with this banquet and ride into the field where the men had stopped their labor exactly at noon each day. Dessert was not a constant of this feast, but Mrs. Remmert's chocolate cake would sometimes become the perfect ending. I have made this cake more than 200 times. My sister-in-law made it for her daughter's wedding at a lavish Napa Valley winery. It simply is the best cake ever. You can double it, triple it, cover it with ganache, sprinkle cocoa powder on it, use it in an ice cream cake, or whatever you would dream up for a chocolate cake. Mrs. Remmert is a farm woman who lives on with this timeless recipe.

Ingredients
1½ C flour
1 C sugar
2 T cocoa powder
1 egg
½ C vegetable oil
1 C warm water
1 t baking soda
¾ t salt
1 t vanilla

Instructions
Dissolve the baking soda in the warm water for 5 minutes as you assemble the rest of the ingredients.
Mix all dry ingredients.
Add wet ingredients and the soda water.
Bake in an 8 x 8 or 9 inch round pan for 22 minutes at 375. (For a double layer cake or 9 x 13, double the recipe.)

Chocolate Miracle Whip Cake with Butter Cream Frosting
Judy Kenna

My mom made this cake every year for my birthday until I started my own family. I even bake it every year for myself. Fond memories.

Ingredients
3¼ C flour
1½ C sugar
2/3 C unsweetened cocoa powder
2¼ t baking powder
1½ t baking soda
1½ C Miracle Whip
1½ C water
1½ t vanilla

Instructions
Mix together all ingredients. Stir until smooth. Bake at 350 for 30 minutes.

Frosting:
1/3 C melted butter
1/8 t salt
3 C powdered sugar
1/8 C milk
1½ t vanilla

Instructions
Mix together all ingredients. Beat until smooth. Spread evenly over cooled cake. Top with chopped pecans if desired.

Mom's Carrot Cake
Virginia K White

I don't remember the first time Mom made this cake, but it was a winner from the "Get Go" so to speak. I was surprised that it was called carrot cake because I couldn't see any carrots and didn't taste any. This has been a favorite in our family for years and is often requested for a birthday cake.

Ingredients

1¼ C oil
2 C flour
1 t salt
4 eggs
3 baby food jars of strained carrots
2 C sugar
2 t soda
2 t cinnamon (I love cinnamon and usually add a bit more)
2 t vanilla

Instructions

Put all dry ingredients together, add liquids, and mix well.
Bake in a 9 x 13 in pan at 350 for about 40 minutes or until the toothpick comes out clean.

Icing:

3 oz. pkg. cream cheese
½ stick of butter
2 t vanilla
2-3 C powdered sugar
Milk

Instructions

Mix together all ingredients. Add milk as needed for the right consistency.
Let cake cool and then frost. I usually keep the cake in the refrigerator.

Anti-Depression Cake
Joe Trey

During COVID, our family decided to tackle Depression Era recipes. We aptly called them Anti-Depression. These were recipes to cheer ourselves up. We made some classics from the depression era and even invented some of our own. We decided that during COVID, calories don't count! Just enjoy!

Ingredients
3½ C all-purpose flour
2 C granulated sugar
2 t baking soda
1 t salt
2 T white vinegar
1 T + 1 t vanilla
2 C water

Instructions
Preheat oven to 375, grease 2 – 9 inch round cake pans.

Add the flour, sugar, baking soda, and salt to a large bowl. Add the water, oil, vinegar, and vanilla. Mix with a whisk until well-blended. Do not over beat. It will still turn out even if there are a few small lumps. Divide batter between the 2 greased cake pans. Bake on a middle rack of oven for 35 minutes or until an inserted toothpick comes out clean.

Frosting:
1-white chocolate pudding or instant pudding of choice
1-C milk
1-container Cool Whip

Instructions
Mix instant pudding with one cup of milk. Refrigerate for an hour or more. (Standard directions will call for more milk. Don't do it. Trust me. It will get soupy and hard to spread.) Fold the Cool Whip into the pudding. Frost one of the cakes. Place the other on top and continue frosting.

Black Midnight Cake
Loreen Hughes

This cake recipe is from my maternal Papa Gene. We like this dry cake because it holds up to a shallow bowl of milk. Best eaten with a big spoon!

Ingredients
2/3 C shortening
1 1/3 C sugar
3 eggs
1¼ C flour
2/3 C cocoa
¼ t baking powder
1¼ t baking soda
1 t salt
1¼ C-water
1 t vanilla

Instructions
Cream together sugar, shortening, and eggs 5 minutes. Mix in dry ingredients alternately with water and vanilla.

Bake 40-45 minutes at 350 in a 9" x 13" pan.

Tom Osborne's Coke Cake
Janet Gabenstein

Tom Osborne, head coach at the University of Nebraska for 25 years, was a legend in the state and talented in many ways. My mom's brother was a scholarship player for the Huskers. He and Tom were about the same age and played together. Tom went to Hastings and my uncle went to the Air Force and then New Jersey. Tom coached under Devaney and Uncle Jim was instrumental in getting some top players to UNL via Monte Kiffin. We met Tom through this link and my grandma always had goodies for him. As a thank you one time, Tom gave this cake recipe to her. I like it because it is unusual and, of course, because of the source. I don't know if this was Tom's recipe, his wife's, or his mother's, but we love it.

I discovered that Tom sometimes exercised at Madonna Pro Active where I exercise. One night before Thanksgiving, Tom and I were the only ones working out. When I got ready to leave, he was waiting at the door and said he would walk me to the car. He asked me if I was doing anything special for Thanksgiving and I said, "Yes, I made your Coke Cake." He burst out laughing.

Ingredients
2 C flour
2 C sugar
½ C butter
½ C vegetable oil
3 T cocoa
1 C Coca Cola
2 eggs
½ C buttermilk
1 t baking soda
1 t vanilla
1½ C mini marshmallows

Instructions
Preheat oven 350.

Combine flour and sugar and set aside. In a saucepan mix butter, oil, cocoa and Coca Cola. Bring to a boil and pour over flour and sugar mixture. Add buttermilk, soda, beaten eggs, vanilla, and marshmallows. Stir by hand until well mixed. Pour into prepared greased 9-13" pan. Bake 30-40 minutes until it tests done. Frost while still warm.

Frosting
½ C butter
3 T cocoa

6 T Coca Cola
1 t vanilla
1 lb. confectioner's sugar
1 C chopped walnuts

Instructions

In saucepan combine butter, cocoa, and Coca Cola. Bring to boil and beat in sugar, vanilla, and nuts until smooth. Spread over warm cake.

Blueberry Cheesecake
Virginia K. White

Home Economics teachers have wonderful recipes! When I taught in Cheyenne, Wyoming, the Home Economics teachers were a short distance from my classroom. When my youngest daughter, Kari, decided she loved cheesecake and wanted to try to make one, I asked for a recipe. Wow! We loved this and made it often.

Crust:
2 C graham cracker crumbs (10 crackers)
1½ t flour
1½ t powdered sugar
½ C melted margarine

Instructions
Combine crumbs, flour and confectioner's sugar. Stir in melted margarine. Press crust mixture firmly on bottom and sides of ungreased 9 inch baking dish.

Filling:
2 pkg. (8 oz each) cream cheese, softened
¾ C sugar
2 t vanilla
2 eggs beaten

Instructions
Cream softened cream cheese and beat in sugar until smooth. Add vanilla and eggs. Spread over the crust and bake at 350 for 15-20 minutes, until set.

Topping:
1 pt. sour cream
2 T sugar
½ t vanilla
1 can (21 oz) Blueberry Fruit filling

Instructions
Blend sour cream, sugar, and vanilla. Spoon over cake immediately upon removing from oven. Return cake to oven for 15 minutes more. Cool cake. Spread Blueberry Fruit Filling over topping. Cover and refrigerate before serving.

Amaretto Cheesecake from the Old Cornhusker Hotel
Janet Grabenstein

This was a popular treat offered by the well-known Cornhusker Hotel in Lincoln, Nebraska. The hotel was demolished and rebuilt many years ago and I don't believe this cheese cake is offered in any of the local restaurants any more. When my high school class graduated, we chartered a train between Lincoln and Omaha as a venue for our class party. It left at midnight and returned as the sun was rising. Most of the class went to the cornhusker and ordered a traditional breakfast. I was the exception. I ordered the cheesecake and they fortunately had one slice left from the night before. When I make this, I always think of the class that day. Leaving the lives we knew in academia, starting over lives in the real world, and thinking about those friends. It seems to signify both the end and the beginning for me.

Ingredients
Crust:
1¼ C graham cracker crumbs
1/3 C softened butter
¼ C brown sugar

Cheesecake:
3 8 oz. pkgs. cream cheese
1 C sugar
3 eggs
2 t vanilla
1 C sour cream
½ C Amaretto

Instructions
Preheat oven to 350. Use an 8 inch spring form pan. Combine all crust ingredients, press into bottom of pan. In a blender, blend cream cheese, vanilla, eggs, sour cream, and blend. Add sugar, then Amaretto and blend once more. Pour into spring form pan on top of graham cracker crust.

Bake 1 hour at 350 until cheesecake is firm in the center. Turn off oven, leave door ajar slightly for 1 hour, and then cool on a rack. Chill in refrigerator overnight. Release from pan, slice, and serve.

Grandma Cederdahl's Rhubarb Cake
Janet Grabenstein

My parents and grandparents were very much into gardening. They had many "fruits of the land" that came up every year. Strawberries, plums, apples, and rhubarb to name a few. Rhubarb was the real announcement of spring for us and we loved rhubarb pies, jams ,stewed rhubarb over ice cream, and the great cake. It was both sweet and tart, making me think of the sweetness of spring taking over the sometimes tartness of a long and cold Nebraska winter. It was the promise of good things to come.

Ingredients
5 C rhubarb cut into small pieces
1 C sugar
1 3 oz. pkg. of raspberry Jell-O
3 C mini marshmallows
1 yellow cake mix, prepared-unbaked

Instructions
Preheat oven to 350.

Spread rhubarb on bottom of a 9 x 13 inch pan. Mix sugar and Jell-O and spread on top of the rhubarb. Add the marshmallows.

Prepare cake mix as directed on package. Spread prepared mix over top of rhubarb and marshmallows.

Bake 1 hour at 350. Let cool and then cut into squares. Serve with whipped topping.

Mom's Marry Me Ice Box Cake
Cheryl Ilov

This recipe is ridiculously simple, especially considering how delicious and irresistible it is. My mother made it for my father when they were still dating, and according to my father, that is the main reason he asked her to marry him. Yes, it really is that good.

However, once they were married my father would often complain that he never got ice box cake anymore. My mother would give him a sultry look, and the next day there would be ice box cake for dessert. After all, that's why my father proposed to her.

But the truth was, my dad decided to marry her from the first moment he set eyes on her at a local dance, when she was only sixteen years old. I can only surmise that it wasn't just the ice box cake that he found so irresistible.

Ingredients

1 box graham crackers
1 4.6 oz. box cook and serve Jell-O chocolate pudding
1 4.6 oz. box cook and serve Jell-O vanilla pudding
Whipped cream or Cool Whip for topping

NOTE: You must use cook and serve pudding. Instant pudding mix will not work.

Instructions

Place one layer of graham crackers in the bottom of a 13" x 9" baking dish. Prepare the chocolate pudding according to directions. While the pudding is still hot, pour it over the graham crackers, and place another layer of graham crackers on top of the pudding. Prepare the vanilla pudding according to directions, pour over the second layer of graham crackers, then place in the refrigerator to chill. Serve with Cool Whip or whipped cream on top.

Raisin Pudding
Elaine Anderson Michaud

This was a favorite of my dad's and I always made it when my mom and dad came over to eat.

Ingredients
½ C brown sugar
½ C milk
1 heaping cup of flour
½ t salt
Butter the size of a walnut (approx. 3 T)
2 t baking powder
½ C raisins
1½ -C boiling water
Butter the size of an egg (1/4 C)
1 –C brown sugar
1-t vanilla

Instructions
Combine first 7 ingredients and set aside.

Combine last 4 ingredients. Bring to boiling point in saucepan. Pour into 8"x 8" baking dish. Drop batter by spoonful into sauce. Bake at 350 for 30 minutes.

Chocolate Mousse (Or French Silk Pie)
Virginia White

This recipe was given to me by a student when I was teaching World Humanities at Eaglecrest. As part of their end of the semester project in the class, they were to provide a little something from the culture they studied. Most students opted to give us a taste of their culture and this was the case here. It was a huge hit with the students and has been a huge hit with my family. When I pulled this recipe out to use it, I noticed that it is rather "seasoned" with the ingredients, thus showing how much I used it.

Ingredients
1 C butter softened
1½ C sugar
3 squares unsweetened chocolate
4 eggs
3 t vanilla

Instructions
Beat butter with sugar until well blended and fluffy. Add melted, cooled chocolate and vanilla. Beat in eggs one at a time, taking 5 minutes to incorporate each egg. Electric mixer should be on medium speed. Eggs MUST be well beaten. I put the mousse into small cups and then chilled them for several hours prior to serving.

Banana Pudding
Gina Sheridan and Flo Francis

Louise Parkinson Evans grew up in southern Arkansas. She was the oldest of five children and learned to cook at an early age. My mother was famous in our county for her biscuits, her vegetables, her fried chicken and catfish, and her desserts. She was definitely a Southern cook and used ingredients that were on hand to a real advantage. I can still taste her fried okra, her turnip greens, fried cornbread, cornbread dressing, homemade rolls and more, but her desserts were always present and some were bigger favorites than others.

My sister, Flo, and I always got to choose what we wanted for dessert for our birthdays. Mother was a great baker of pies and cakes, but there was always one dessert that both of us usually chose for our birthday dessert. I still make this dessert the way Mother did. I make the custard from scratch because it just seems to be better than the quick instant kind. Believe me, there is a difference!

Ingredients
1 egg
¾ C sugar
3 T flour
¼ t salt
2 C milk
1 t vanilla
6 bananas
1 box of Nilla Wafers

Instructions
Make the custard first. Beat the egg slightly and add the sifted dry ingredients. Slowly add milk and cook over low heat until thick. Stir constantly. Remove from heat and add vanilla. Set aside.

Choose a dessert bowl for this dessert. The bowl is a special ingredient for my sister, Flo, and me. Mother had two such bowls. I would call them a soufflé bowl today. When my mother died, Flo and I went through all of her things, and both of us wanted the "banana pudding" bowl. Lucky for us, Mother had two identical bowls she used for this dessert. To this day, we both make it only in this bowl.

In your bowl, line the bottom with vanilla wafers, next slices of the bananas, then half of the pudding. Create another layer of wafers, and the pudding. Crumble the remaining wafers and sprinkle on the top. Cover lightly and refrigerate.

Some recipes for banana pudding call for a meringue topping or even Cool Whip. This one focuses on making a really flavorful custard. There is no need for the big toppings.

And, take it from my sister and me, this dessert is a perfect one to eat anytime of the day or night. It just cries out for a spoon!

Rugelah
Yael Abrahamsson

I found this recipe as I was sorting through my mother-in-law's recipe books and folders. She learned to cook from her own mother-in-law and my husband learned from both of his grandmothers. My mother-in-law was a terrific cook by the time I knew her, and her desserts were great too. Since my husband's the cook in the family, I have been working through some of her baking recipes. This one's a winner. From what I gather, most rugelach in the US is made with cream cheese dough. This one is more old world, I think. You'll want to make the dough the night before you want to bake these, though you could probably make the dough in the morning and bake later in the day.

Dough Ingredients
1 stick butter, softened
1½ T sugar
½ C sour cream plus ½ t vinegar (white vinegar is best)
1 egg yolk (reserve the white for brushing later)
1½ C all-purpose flour
1 package dry yeast (2 ¼ t active dry yeast)

Dough Directions
Cream together the butter and sugar until light and fluffy. Add the rest of the ingredients and mix until well blended. (I know, it seems strange, but just add them all to the mixer bowl and mix together.) Once the dough has come together, form it into a ball. Brush it with a bit of melted butter and wrap it in plastic wrap. Refrigerate it overnight. I just cover a little dish with the unused egg white and put it in the refrigerator for the next day.

Filling Option #1 Ingredients
¾ C sugar
1 t cinnamon
½ cup, up to 2/3 cup pecans - toasted (grind them in a food processor)
½ cup, up to 2/3 cup chocolate (optional, in place of the pecans)
Melted butter (2-4 T)

Instructions
Preheat oven to 375.
Take the dough out of the refrigerator. Divide in two and return one half to the fridge while you work with the first half.
Roll the half of dough into a circle—should be 12 inches in diameter.

Brush the circle of dough with melted butter, sprinkle with the cinnamon sugar and ground pecans. Cut the circle into 24 small triangles. Roll each small triangle from the wider, outside end in to form a crescent. Place on baking sheet (use parchment paper as these will leak.) Brush with egg white and bake 13-15 minutes or until golden brown. Remove from heat, let cool a few minutes and remove from cookie sheet. Repeat process with the rest of the dough.

Filling Option 2
2/3 C jam (I like apricot the best; raspberry is also good, but really you can use what you like)
2 T sugar
½ t cinnamon

Instructions
Roll out the dough as above.
Heat the jam to make it liquid.
Brush a thin layer of jam over the circle of dough. Then sprinkle with cinnamon sugar and ground pecans or chocolate. Cut and roll and bake as above.

Note 1: It's mess to cut and roll the crescents – this is not a tidy recipe!
Note 2: You can experiment with other fillings.

Cherry Dream Bars
Judy Kenna

This has been a family favorite for many years. The kids especially enjoy getting their hands in the crust and squishing the butter with the flour and sugar.

Pastry Ingredients
2 C flour
1 C butter
3/8 C powdered sugar

Pastry Instructions
Mix with hands until smooth. Spread into 13" x 9" pan. Bake at 350 for 20-25 minutes until light brown around the edges.

Topping Ingredients
4 eggs
2 C sugar
½ t salt
½ C flour
1 t baking powder
2 t vanilla
1 C finely chopped cherries
1 C shredded coconut
1½ C chopped nuts

Topping and Assembly Instructions
Mix all ingredients and spread on warm pastry. Bake for 22 minutes. Wait until completely cool to cut into small bars.

Italian Spumoni Bars
Judy Kenna

I started making these cookies when I was about 10 years old. It was in a magazine as a basic recipe that could be made into 100 different cookies. That year I made about 20 different kinds but this is the one that I continue to make every year.

These are two of the recipes that are included in my Christmas baking every year. My family and I bake over 25 kinds of cookies and candy every Christmas to give to family and friends. My husband, two kids, their spouses, and all 6 of my grandkids work with us for a week to create these cookie plates. Such a special family time and memories are created every year.

Ingredients

1 C butter
1½ C powdered sugar
2½ C flour
1 t vanilla
1 egg

Instructions

Blend the ingredients and divide into 3 parts.

To first part add 3 oz melted chocolate chips. To second part add ½ C chopped nuts and green food coloring. To third part add 2 t almond extract and red food coloring.

Form each part into a 3" strip and stack them to form a loaf of chocolate, green, and red. Refrigerate and cut into 1/8 inch slices and bake for 5-7 minutes at 350.

Brown Sugar Cookies
Elaine Michaud

These were always our traditional cut-out Christmas cookies. The brown sugar makes them so much different than the usual sugar cookies. And the kids love "painting" them.

Ingredients
2 C brown sugar
2/3 C shortening
2 eggs, well beaten
1/2 t vanilla
3 C flour
1 t baking powder
Powdered Sugar (for rolling out cookies)

Instructions
Cream together brown sugar and shortening and beat until light and fluffy. Add eggs and vanilla and beat well. Sift together flour and baking powder. Add sifted dry ingredients to creamed mixture. Shape into mound. Wrap in waxed paper and chill thoroughly.

Roll on board lightly floured with powdered sugar until dough is about ¼" thick. Dip cutter in powdered sugar each time before cutting cookies, then place cookies on lightly greased baking sheet.

Bake at 375 for about 8 minutes or until delicately browned.

Flouring with powdered sugar instead of flour is a new trick to prevent toughening of cookies. It prevents sticking and also sweetens the cookie.

To decorate, we use egg yolk paint. Blend 1 egg yolk and ¼ t water. Divide among several small custard cups, depending on how many different colors you wish to use. Add food coloring to each cup for desired color. Paint designs on cookies with small paint brushes. Use a separate brush for each color.

Grandma Cederdahl's Sugar Cookies
Janet Grabenstein

Even though this was a mainstay at Christmas, my grandma made these all of the time. She won several prizes for them. I think she thought a little sugar just makes life sweeter all around. Many people in Lincoln and around the country area knew they'd get a box of her sugar cookies at Christmas time. She never decorated them. When I think of these cookies, I think of Mary Poppins—"a spoonful of sugar makes the medicine go down."

Ingredients
2 eggs
2 sticks of butter
1 C cooking oil
1 t almond flavoring
5½ C-sifted flour
1 t soda
1 C powdered sugar
1 C granulated sugar
1 T vanilla
1 t cream of tarter
1 t salt

Instructions
Cream the butter and sugar together, beat in eggs, add the oil, almond flavoring, and vanilla.

Sift together the flour, cream of tarter, salt, and soda. Add this to the creamed mixture. Leave in refrigerator overnight.

Form dough in cookie size balls and place on greased cookie sheet, then press down with the bottom of a glass dipped in granulated sugar. Sprinkle sugar on each cookie.

Bake at 350 for 12-13 minutes.

More Grandma Cederdahl Specialities Seven Layer Bars
Janet Grabenstein

These and the chocolate cookies were always available at Grandma's house as well as many other varieties of cookies. These cookies are a reminder of surprises sent from Grandma's kitchen.

Ingredients
1 stick margarine (slice into squares)
1 C graham cracker crumbles
1 C shredded coconut
1 6 oz. pkg. chocolate chips
1 6 oz. pkg. butterscotch chips
1 can Eagle Brand condensed milk
1 C shopped pecans

Instructions
Preheat oven to 350 and grease a 9 x 13 pan.
Make layers using the 7 items listed above in the greased 9 x 13 pan. Layer in the order listed.
Bake 25 minutes. Let cool and then cut into bars.

Chocolate Cookies
Janet Grabenstein

Ingredients
½ C butter
½ C Crisco (solid)
1½ C granulated sugar
2 eggs
4 squares melted chocolate
1 C milk
2 T vanilla
3½ C flour
1 t soda
1 t salt
½ C chopped nuts

Instructions
Cream the butter, Crisco, and sugar together. Add the eggs, melted chocolate, milk, and vanilla.
Sift together the flour, soda, and salt. Add the nuts.
Mix the ingredients together, alternating the dry and wet with equal addition of each until combined.
Drop by a spoonful onto baking sheet.
Bake at 400 for 8-10 minutes.
You can frost these with the recipe of powdered sugar chocolate frosting on the side of the Hershey's Cocoa can.

Date Nut Bars
Dawn Vaughn

I make this every Christmas and am reminded of my grandmother each time I bake them. The recipe is so old that liquid oil didn't exist and bakers used words like "slow" or "hot" oven to describe the heat to use. It wouldn't be Christmas without these bars!

Ingredients
4 eggs

2 C confectioners' sugar

2 T shortening, melted (I just use liquid oil)

½ C sifted cake flour

½ t salt

1 t baking powder

2 C chopped dates (you can buy them already chopped)

1½ C chopped nuts (I use pecans)

2 T vanilla

Instructions
Beat eggs until light. Add sugar and shortening. Blend well. Sift dry ingredients together and add dates, nuts, and vanilla. Blend well and pour into greased shallow pan (I use a 9" x 13" pan). Bake in a slow oven (325) about 40 minutes. Cut into bars and roll in confectioners' sugar. Makes 2-2½ dozen.

A Shout Out to the Irish
Irish Cream Brownies
Virginia White

I discovered this recipe when I was teaching in Cheyenne. I think one of my students was doing a fund raiser and I bought a book from her. I have made this every Christmas since my days in Cheyenne and it is always a favorite. Careful so you don't get more Irish Cream in you than in the brownies.

Ingredients
2 oz. unsweetened baking chocolate
½ C butter
1 C sugar
2 eggs, well beaten
1 T Irish whiskey
2/3 C flour
¼ t salt
2/3 C semisweet chocolate chips (opt. but I always put them in)
7 T Irish cream liqueur
1 C confectioners' sugar
3 T butter, softened
Chopped nuts (optional but I always use pecans)

Instructions
Melt chocolate with ½ cup butter in double boiler or microwave. Mix well. Cool. Beat sugar with eggs in bowl. Add whiskey and cooled chocolate mixture; mix well. Stir in flour, salt, and chocolate chips. Pour into greased (use cooking spray) 8' x 8' baking pan. Bake at 325 for 20 minutes or until brownies test done. Cool for 2 hours or longer. Pierce with toothpick. Drizzle 3 tablespoons liqueur over brownies. Combine confectioners' sugar, 3 tablespoons butter and 4 tablespoons liqueur in bowl. Mix well. Spread over brownies. Sprinkle with nuts. Cut into squares.

Katherine's Biscotti
Katherine McIver

I make these every year at Christmas and give them to friends as gifts. They are always a big hit. You can dip the finished biscotti in come melted chocolate or just leave plain. They are tasty and simple to make.

Ingredients
3 C all-purpose flour
4 t baking powder
1 C sugar (can use granulated or brown sugar)
7 T unsalted butter at room temperature
1 t vanilla
3 large eggs at room temperature
¾ C roughly chopped almonds
2 T grated fresh ginger (you can also use orange zest)

Instructions
Preheat oven at 350; lightly flour a 12' x 15' baking sheet.

Sift the flour and baking powder into a medium bowl.

Beat sugar and butter in a large bowl until blended (or use an electric mixer). Add eggs, one at a time, beating until fluffy. Mix in the ginger and almonds. Add flour mixture and beat until well blended.

Divide the dough into 3 parts and shape each into a long, slightly flat log (3 x 12 inches approximately).

Place the logs, 4 inches apart, on the baking sheet and bake for 15 minutes until golden brown. Remove from oven, transfer to a cutting board and slice each loaf diagonally into ½ inch slices. Return the slices cut side down onto the baking sheet.

Bake again for 5 minutes; turn over and bake another 5 minutes. Cookies will be brown on both sides. Cool completely on a cooking rack.

Grandma Cookies
Virginia White

I love reading recipes. I am especially interested in old recipes and I inherited many from my mom's recipe box. One day I was looking for a cookie recipe that I thought the grandkids might like and I found a Sour Cream Cookie recipe. I thought it looked good, but it was an old one. The card was yellow and sprinkled with a few ingredients. I was a little unsure of some of the ingredients, but decided to experiment and see what happened. Needless to say, my experiment turned into a success and my oldest granddaughter, Sheridan, started calling them Grandma Cookies and it stuck! These are frequently requested by every family member and I have been asked for the recipe when I take them to a gathering.

Ingredients
1 3/4 C sugar
1 C margarine
1 C cultured sour cream
4½ C flour (this takes some beating, but be sure to use at least this much and work the flour in)
2 eggs
1 t baking soda
½ t salt (no amount was listed and I decided on ½ teaspoon.)
2 t baking powder
2 t vanilla (the recipe calls for flavoring and I used vanilla)

Instructions
There were no directions regarding the temperature to cook and I finally figured out 325 for 12 minutes worked best. I also figured out that it is best to chill the dough for a while before baking.

I decided to roll the dough into balls and then roll them in a sugar and cinnamon mixture. That was a huge hit. The cookies are like a soft snickerdoodle cookie.

Slimmy's Sour Cream Cookies
Joe Trey

Slimmy (Carrie Jo Wagner) was a tall and slender woman born in the 1800s. Her husband, Buck, was built, like well, a Buck! I suspect Slimmy got her name from standing next to Buck. I guess she made and shared more of these cookies than she ever ate. During COVID, calories don't count, so we chose to enjoy them often. My mother still reminisces about receiving the cookies as care packages, layered and wrapped in waxed paper inside a tin.

Ingredients
2½ C flour
1 t baking powder
½ t baking soda
¼ t salt
1 egg
1 C sugar
½ C shortening or butter
8 oz. carton of sour cream
½ t vanilla
Topping: sugar, nutmeg (mix as much or as little as you want)

Instructions
Sift flour, baking powder, soda, and salt together. Cream shortening with sugar – add the egg and mix well. Alternately add dry ingredients and sour cream into the sugar mixture and continue to mix all ingredients until they are mixed well. Then add vanilla. Drop by a spoonful of dough onto parchment paper covered cookie sheet. Sprinkle top to cookies with sugar and nutmeg mixture
Bake at 400 for 10 minutes

Note: Cookies will be soft and spongy. Do NOT overcook or they lose their yumminess!

Gluten-Free Chocolate Chip Cookies
Yael Abrahamsson

I love to bake and am always looking for something new. I recently found this recipe in the New York Times while looking for something I could make for friends who requested gluten-free cookies. These were a hit. The cookies are tasty. The almond flour gives just a slightly nutty flavor, and they're chewy. One of my tasters said they thought the chocolate could be decreased a little bit. I used bittersweet chocolate, which is a great combination with almond. Part of what was so good is that there are not overly sweet.

Ingredients
2¾ C almond flour
¾ t kosher salt
½ t baking soda
10 T unsalted butter, at room temperature
½ C light brown sugar
½ C granulated sugar
1 large egg
1½ vanilla
12 oz. bittersweet feves or chips, or coarsely chopped bar chocolate
Sea salt, for finishing (optional)

Instructions
Preheat oven to 350. Line two baking sheets with parchment paper.

In a medium bowl, whisk the almond flour, salt, and baking soda to combine.

Cream the butter, brown sugar, and granulated sugar on medium speed until very light, 3-4 minutes. Add the egg and mix on medium speed to combine. Scrape the bowl well, then add the vanilla and mix to combine. Add the dry ingredients and mix on low speed until just combined, about 10 seconds. Scrape the bowl well and mix on low speed to ensure the mixture is homogenous. Add the chocolate and gently mix to incorporate it. Scoop the dough into mounds the size of generous golf balls, and transfer them to the prepared baking sheets. Stagger the rows to allow the cookies room to spread.

Gently press the cookies down slightly with your fingers until about 1½" thick. Sprinkle lightly with sea salt, if using. Bake the cookies, switching racks and rotating the sheets halfway through, until they're golden brown around the edges and just barely set in the center, 18-22 minutes. Transfer sheets to a wire rack for 10 minutes, then transfer cookies with a spatula onto another rack to cool a bit more.

Apricot and Pecan Cookies
Loreen Hughes

These shortbread/butter cookies are, in my opinion, the most underrated type of cookie. These are best eaten warm when the nuts are fragrantly toasty and the apricot is chewy, making these an absolute delight to eat!

Ingredients

1 C butter, softened
¾ C superfine sugar
1 egg yolk, lightly beaten
2 t vanilla
2 C all-purpose flour
Pinch of salt
Finely grated rind of 1 orange
½ C plumped dried apricots, chopped
1/3 C pecans, finely chopped.

Instructions

Place the butter and sugar in a large bowl and beat together until light and fluffy, then beat in the egg yolk and vanilla extract. Sift together the flour and salt into the mixture, add the orange rind and apricots, and stir until combined. Shape the dough into a log. Spread out the pecans in a shallow dish. Roll the log in the nuts until well coated, then wrap in plastic wrap and chill in the refrigerator for 30-60 minutes.

Preheat the oven to 375. Line 2 large baking sheets with parchment paper. Unwrap the dough, cut into ¼ inch slices with a sharp serrated knife, and place the slices on the baking sheets, spaced well apart.

Bake in the preheated oven for 10-12 minutes, or until golden brown. Let cool on the baking sheets for 5-10 minutes, then transfer the cookies to wire racks to cool completely.

Ice Box Cookies
Patricia Winter

My grandmother lived in Independence, Kansas. My family lived in Omaha. About twice a year, we would drive down to visit Grandma. I was her youngest grandchild. As soon as I was in the door, I would run to the kitchen to see if Grandma had refrigerator cookies in her clear glass cookie jar. She always did. I could never get enough.

Ingredients
1 C brown sugar
1 C white sugar
1 C melted Crisco
3 eggs well beaten
3½ C flour
1½ t baking soda
1 t cinnamon
½ t nutmeg
1 t cloves
1 C chopped nut meats
¼ t salt
1 t vanilla

Instructions
Beat eggs, sugar, and Crisco.

Add vanilla. Stir in the dry ingredients and the nuts.

Mix all together and make into 4 rolls and put in wax paper and place in ice box until chilled thoroughly. Cut in thin slices and bake with oven temperature at 450 (this is from the original recipe. No time is listed. Recollection is 4-5 minutes) Current temperatures and times for a similar recipe indicate 350 for 10-12 minutes.

Grandma's Reindeer Cookies
Taylor A. Ilov

Making reindeer cookies with my grandma was an annual Christmas tradition that I shared with my brother and three cousins. Every December, as soon as the Christmas decorations were up, Grandma would set a day for all of us to come over to her house and bake cookies.

We made an entire day of it, and would often go sled riding first because Grandma and Grandpa had the best yard for sledding. Besides, Grandma loved watching us through the window, and sometimes she laughed so hard that it looked like she was having more fun than we were. Grandpa watched as well, but for some reason, he always had some place he needed to go when we came back inside.

That's when the real fun started. Grandma was very particular about what she wanted us to do and gave us very specific instructions. Not everyone listened to her, but I always did because I wanted my cookies to be perfect. And they were. Grandma also had a wicked sense of humor, and when the reindeer cookies came out of the oven, she told us they looked like a row of little bare baby bottoms. That observation was greeted with high pitched squeals of *"Grandma!"*

Grandma is gone, but her famous reindeer cookies live on. Every Christmas, after decorations go up, my mom, brother, and I gather in the kitchen to make reindeer cookies and share Grandma stories. However, no matter how hard we try, we just can't see little bare baby bottoms in the cookies. But don't worry, we'll continue to keep looking.

Ingredients
1½ C butter or margarine
1½ C peanut butter
1½ C brown sugar
1½ C white sugar
3 eggs
5 C flour
1½ t baking powder
2½ t baking soda
Red and Green M & Ms
Mini pretzels

Instructions
Combine margarine, peanut butter, white sugar, brown sugar, eggs and cream well. Add flour, baking powder, and baking soda. Refrigerate dough for 1 hour.

Make one-inch balls and place on lightly greased cookie sheet. Using a flat bottom glass, press down. Add 2 small pretzels for antlers, add M & Ms for eyes and a nose.

Bake 8-10 minutes at 350.

Bespoke Shortbread Cookies
Lynn Evenson

I gave this shortbread recipe the name "bespoke" because I've made it with several different flavor profiles. This is a favorite because it's insanely good for very little effort and also because my husband, Erik, loves shortbread. Too, it has a very deep connection with Scotland, a place we've come to love. Also, since *Cook's Illustrated* baking book has fine-tuned it, their recipe avoids pitfalls like undissolved sugar and tough texture. I've made the cardamom and lemon version. Potentially you might make lime, orange, or ginger.

Ingredients
½ C old-fashioned oats
1½ C all-purpose flour
¼ C cornstarch
2/3 C confectioner's sugar
½ t salt
14 T (1 and ¾ sticks) unsalted butter-- chilled and coarsely chopped

Instructions
Pulse oats in spice grinder or something similar until reduced to a fine powder; you should have ¼ to 1/3 Cup.

Using stand mixer fitted with paddle, mix oat flour, all-purpose flour, cornstarch, sugar, and salt until well combined – 5-10 seconds. Add butter and mix just until dough forms (sort of—it may not coalesce, so feel free to add a little more butter if this happens) 5-10 minutes. Adjust oven rack to middle position and heat oven to 450.

On a parchment paper lined baking sheet, place the locked collar of a 9" x 9 ½" spring form pan, upside down (you won't need the bottom piece). Press dough into this collar at ½ " thickness, smoothing with the back of a large spoon. Using a 2" diameter biscuit cutter, remove the middle of the disc of dough, and put it on the parchment paper alongside the collar. Unlock the collar, but leave it in place.

Bake for 5 minutes then, reduce oven temp to 250. Bake until edges turn pale gold, 10-15 minutes. Remove baking sheet from oven and turn oven off. Remove spring form collar. With a sharp chef's knife, score the dough into 16 wedges, cutting about halfway through. With a toothpick, poke a number of holes in each wedge (5-10). Return to oven and prop the door open about 1". Let the shortbread dry about an hour until center is pale gold, too. Shortbread should be firm but giving to touch.

Transfer sheet to cooling rack and allow to cool to room temp. Cut at score marks before serving.

Notes: If you are appalled at the use of this much butter, you can substitute low-fat mayonnaise for half of it.

You can toast the oats before grinding them if you like that taste better. You don't even have to grind these, but it will change the texture a bit. Stir them in as directed above.

If you decide to use cardamom, add a tablespoon of coarsely ground cardamom to the recipe.

For lemon, you can add ¼ to 1/3 teaspoon lemon juice and about 3 tablespoons grated lemon zest when you add the butter.

You can also add ½ cup chopped crystallized ginger instead of lemon.

Sugar and Cinnamon Pretzels
Marilyn Ferguson

One of my best friends shared these with me two years ago and I fell in love with them. I hope you enjoy them as much as I do.

Ingredients
9 oz. bag of pretzels
2/3 C vegetable oil
½ C sugar
2 t cinnamon

Instructions
Mix until coated, then microwave (1/2 batch) at a time for 3 minutes on high, stirring every minute. Spread out on waxed paper. Cool. Delicious!

Milk "n" Cookies Fudge
Marilyn Ferguson

My daughter and her friend, Wendy, try to do cookie baking and candy making each December. This is one of their favorites.

Ingredients
3 C white chocolate chips
1 T butter
Pinch of Kosher salt
1 t pure vanilla extract
1 C sweetened condensed milk
1½ C Marshmallow Fluff
1 C mini chocolate chips
1 C crushed mini chocolate chips cookies
½ C mini chocolate chip cookies

Instructions
Line square 9 x 9 pan with parchment paper and then grease with cooking spray.

In a small saucepan over medium heat, combine white chocolate chips, sweetened condensed milk, butter, vanilla, and salt. Cook, stirring often, until melted and smooth. Reduce heat to medium low and add Marshmallow Fluff. Stir until melted. Remove from heat and immediately stir in mini chocolate chips and crushed mini chocolate chip cookies.

Pour mixture into prepared baking pan and immediately press whole mini chocolate chip cookies into fudge. 2-3 hours and then slice into squares.

Chocolate Crinkles
Rosette Obedoza

Crinkles are a popular type of drop cookie in the Philippines during the holidays. This recipe was given to me by my younger sister, Roselle, and has become a favorite cookie recipe of mine during the holiday cookie exchange events – plus, who doesn't love chocolate? I am older by 10 years and I remember teaching Roselle how to bake. I am proud of the woman and mother she has become. Her love for cookies and baking continues as she experiments with varying cuisine and recipe books. She is now officially a better baker than I am!

Ingredients
¾ C butter
1 C granulated white sugar
1 C packed brown sugar
3 eggs
1 t vanilla
1½ C all-purpose flour
1 C cocoa powder
¼ C buttermilk
1 T baking powder
1 t baking soda
Powdered sugar to sprinkle on top of crinkles

Instructions
Preheat oven to 350.

Cream butter with both the white and brown sugar. Beat in eggs, vanilla, and buttermilk. Sift together dry ingredients and blend into the creamed mixture. Drop by rounded teaspoons onto a greased baking sheet and bake for 13-15 minutes. Allow cookies to cool on the sheet and remove when they are firm. Using a strainer, sprinkle top of crinkles with powdered sugar.

Peanut Brittle
Dawn Pemberton Vaughn

My granddad made this recipe every year while I was growing up. It is my favorite recipe for peanut brittle.

Ingredients
2 C sugar
1 C corn syrup
½ C water
Boil until you reach 240 degrees (230 in Denver)

Instructions
Add 3 cups raw peanuts and boil while stirring constantly (sometimes I need a book while doing this) until it reaches 320 degrees (310 in Denver).

Immediately put 1 teaspoon butter and vanilla and 2 teaspoons baking soda. Those should be measured out in advance. Beat the mixture until everything is dissolved. Pour out onto greased cookie sheet and let cool. Do not spread as it will make the brittle tough.

Bavarian Mints
Margie Smith

This is a copy-cat of the original Bavarian mints from the House of Bauer in Lincoln, Nebraska. It is a favorite of my family and many others in Nebraska as well as the Midwest.

Ingredients
12 oz package semi-sweet chocolate chips melted
1 T butter, melted
1 14 oz. can sweetened condensed milk
1 t vanilla
4 drops cream de mint extract

Instructions
Mix all ingredients together. Spread onto a greased 9 x 13 sheet pan. Refrigerate until firm. Cut into bite size pieces.

A Little Nod to Trisha Yearwood and Garth Brooks
Graham Cracker Brittle
Janet Grabenstein

I was president of a national nonprofit a number of years ago and was invited almost everywhere in the U.S. to speak. Interestingly, along the way, I met several celebrities, two of which were Trisha Yearwood and Garth Books. As I began visiting in the various towns, food always seemed to become part of our conversations because I was visiting the home areas of the celebrities. This is one of the recipes that came into the conversations I had with Trisha Yearwood and Garth Books. It is a little salty and a little sweet, just like life. Easy to make and gets enjoyed way too fast – then – you just have to make more.

Ingredients
Graham crackers - enough to cover the baking sheet
1 C brown sugar
1½ C pecans, broken
1 stick of butter

Instructions
Cover a cookie sheet with foil. Lay out graham crackers to cover the cookie sheet.
Mix brown sugar, pecans, and butter. Bring to a boil for 2 minutes.
Pour mixture over crackers. Bake 7 minutes at 350. Let cool and then break into pieces.

Note: You can substitute saltines for a different taste and you can also drizzle the saltine and pecan brittle with melted chocolate after it cools and before you break it up.

Homemade Easy Carmel Corn
Cheryl Townsley

I make MANY batches ahead of time and store in a big trash bag. Then, I put them into decorative bags, tins, or jars, and decorate.

Ingredients
7 oz. popped popcorn
¾ C maple syrup
1/3 C butter
3 T organic brown sugar (or coconut sugar)
½ t salt
½ t vanilla
¼ t baking soda

Instructions
Preheat oven to 300.
Pour the popped popcorn into clean sink (stop up drain so nothing can be lost).
Combine syrup, butter, sweetener, and salt into a heavy pan and melt together.
Without stirring, let gently boil for 3-4 minutes.
Remove from heat and add vanilla and baking soda.
Pour syrup over popcorn and mix until evenly coated.
Place on oiled cookie sheet with sides (jelly roll pan).
Bake at 300 degrees for 15 minutes.
Cool and put into containers.

Mashed Potato Candy
Elaine Michaud

Every year at Christmas my grandma Peckham made all kinds of candy, wrapped them in greeting card boxes (remember those?) and mailed them to her nine daughters and their families. This mashed potato candy was my very favorite. Don't knock until you try it!

Ingredients
¾ C cold mashed potatoes
4 C confectioner's sugar
4 C shredded coconut
1½ t vanilla
½ t salt
8 squares baking chocolate

Instructions
Mix potatoes, confectioner's sugar, coconut, vanilla, and salt and spread into a large pan so it will be about ½ inch thick. Melt chocolate over hot water, but do not let the water boil. Spread the melted chocolate on top of the candy. Cool. Cut into squares.

Mom's Toffee
Virginia White

My mother made this every Christmas! I could hardly wait. She made so many cookies and different kinds of candy, but this was, by far, my favorite as well as a favorite of my husband and daughters. She always made enough to gift many people and people raved about it.

Ingredients
2 C sugar
2 C butter and margarine (I use half and half)
6 T water
2 T white corn syrup

Instructions
Boil above ingredients to the hard crack stage, using a candy thermometer (300 degrees).

Butter your cookie sheet well before starting to cook the toffee. Place broken pieces of Hershey bars and pecans or almonds on the bottom of the pan. Save some for the top of the toffee. Let harden and then break into pieces. *This can be kept in an air-tight container for several months.

NOTE: My family would not know if that would work because it never lasted that long.

Popcorn Balls
Connie Hirz

My parents made popcorn balls for Christmas every year. They would put each one in a sandwich size plastic bag and tie it with red or green ribbon. There was a big basket filled with popcorn balls by the front door and anyone who stopped by to visit could take a few. Enlist one or two people to help you form these while the candy part is still warm. It will become a tradition!

Ingredients

2/3 C white Karo Syrup
2 C sugar
2/3 C water
½ t salt
1 cube butter
1 t vanilla
1 pound popcorn popped

Instructions

Combine Karo syrup, sugar, water, and salt in a heavy pan. Stir to blend and boil until mixture spins a thread. (230 degrees on candy thermometer.) REMOVE FROM HEAT, add 1 cube butter and 1 tsp. vanilla.

Pour mixture over popcorn. Stir with buttered wooden spoon. Let mixture cool for approximately 2 or 3 minutes. With buttered hands form into baseball sized balls.

Knutson Family Ice Cream
Dede Stockton

This recipe was passed down for generations. Use an ice cream freezer with plenty of ice cream salt and ice. Making this ice cream brings back memories of my childhood and family gatherings! All the kids would take turns sitting on the freezer while the "men" would crank the handle on our old ice cream freezer. Of course, I use an electric one now, but the flavor is still the same. We make a point of churning our ice cream several times each summer and the whole family anticipates the great flavor. **Note:** Because I have several lactose intolerant people in my family, I now use lactose free milk to make everyone happy, and the flavor is just as amazing!

Ingredients
4 eggs
1¾ C sugar
½ t salt
3 T flour
1 can Carnation milk
1 can Eagle Brand milk
3 T vanilla
½ gallon whole milk

Instructions
Beat eggs well, add salt, sugar, and flour and 1 quart milk. Cook until thickened, stirring constantly. Pour the mixture through strainer and into freezer container. Add vanilla and milk to 1" from top of container. Freeze. Store in your freezer until ready to eat.

Burnett Family Ice Cream
Virginia White

The Burnett family served ice cream at every Thanksgiving and Christmas dinner. There were usually other desserts, but ice cream was the favorite. I would rather have that than cake or pie. When I went through Mom's recipes, I discovered she actually had two different recipes, but the second one was when she decided to make a chocolate chip version. I think she and my aunt also figured out how to add strawberries and other fruits to the ice cream. My favorite, of course, was the chocolate chip version. Adding a small amount of water to the top of the ice and salt mixture will speed up the freezing process. This was my Granddad Burnett's secret because he could not wait all of that time for it to start freezing—especially when he was turning a freezer by hand. I remember being part of that and then we were all thrilled when we were able to get an electric freezer.

Ingredients
3½ C whipping cream
5 eggs
3 C sugar
1 t salt
2 T vanilla (Watkins or more if imitation)
4 C whole milk (or enough to fill the canister to within 1 to 1 and ½ inches of the top.

Instructions
Whip cream in a large bowl until thick, but not thick enough to serve as a topping. Beat whole eggs and gradually add sugar, vanilla, and salt. Add to cream, then add whole milk, 2 or 3 cups at first. Pour into canister. Now, continue to add the rest of the whole milk (usually 4 cups or more to reach the 1 to 1 and ½ inches of top. The whipping and beating of ingredients before actual freezing cuts down on the freezing time.

In freezing, add a thick layer of crushed ice, followed by a generous amount of rock salt, alternating until the freezer is entirely covered. I add about ½ C of water to start the freezing process.

This is a rich ice cream and will not crystalize if taken immediately from freezer and put in an air tight, cold container.

To make chocolate chip ice cream: Heat and melt 4 squares of unsweetened chocolate or 2 oz to a square. Add hot chocolate to cream mixture with a fork, a small portion at a time and be careful to stir as you pour into the canister and even after all milk has been added, using a long spoon. Freeze immediately by following the directions above.

Crockpot Applesauce
Connie Hirz

With several apple trees in our Wheat Ridge, Colorado, backyard, I was always looking for recipes that used apples. I found this and it became a family favorite because the aroma of cinnamon and apples filled our home. It's easy and delicious and perfect on a crisp, fall day.

Ingredients
8 medium apples – nice to use a combination of apples.
1 t fresh lemon juice
3 inch cinnamon stick
5 t light brown sugar
Peel, core, and slice apples

Instructions
Place in slow cooker. Add the cinnamon stick, lemon, and brown sugar.
Set crockpot to low and cook for 6 hours. Stir apples occasionally. Remove cinnamon stick and use an immersion blender to blend until smooth. If you prefer a chunky applesauce, leave sauce intact.

Kids' Korner
Cooking and Creating

"I do not like
Green eggs and ham
I do not like them,
Sam-I-am"
From Green Eggs and Ham
Dr. Seuss

Mixing up pancakes

Family Holiday cookie decorating

Icing cupcakes

Mixing up something good

Baking with kids

Tracy's Yum Deluxe
Tracy Bowersox

When I was homeschooling my two boys, we did some projects in the kitchen. One day I gave them an assignment to create a special cream pie. My oldest created The Great Graham which got only so-so reviews because the Golden Grahams he mixed in got soggy. My youngest created Tracy's Yum Deluxe which I've made him for his birthday almost every year since.

Ingredients
1 chocolate cookie crumb crust (6 oz)
1 box chocolate pudding (4 oz)
1¾ C milk
3 oz. cream cheese, softened
6-8 Reese's Peanut Butter cups—chopped
Whipped Topping

Instructions
Gradually beat milk into cream cheese until smooth. Add pudding mix and beat according to package directions. Mix in ½ of the chopped peanut butter cups. Swirl in ½ cup whipped topping. Pour into crust. Chill until firm. Add more whipped topping on top and sprinkle with remaining peanut butter cups.

Easy Peasy Lemon Cookies
Margie Smith

My sister-in-law, Margie Smith, gave me this recipe quite some time ago and it has been a fun one to make with the grandkids. We have even tried it with other cake mix flavors. It's easy and teaches measurements and following directions.

Ingredients
1 lemon cake mix
2 eggs
1/3 C vegetable oil
1 t lemon extract
2/3 C powdered sugar

Instructions
Preheat oven to 350

Mix all ingredients. Form dough into balls. You might have to add a little flour in order to have the right consistency for dough balls. Roll balls in powdered sugar.

Bake 6-9 minutes on ungreased cookie sheet. Let cool 5 minutes before removing from pan.

NOTE: Sometimes we have rolled the dough in cinnamon and sugar rather than powdered sugar.

White Chocolate Ting-a-Lings
Marilyn Ferguson

My granddaughter, Kelsey, has made these with me for Christmas since she was 3 years old. It is one of her favorites.

Ingredients
3½ C Chow Mein noodles
3½ C salted cocktail peanuts
32 oz. white chocolate candy coating
Sprinkles

Instructions
Mix Chow Mein noodles and peanuts in a large bowl. Melt white chocolate until smooth and pour over Chow Mein noodles and peanuts. Mix well. Drop by spoonfuls onto wax paper and sprinkle with your favorite sprinkles.

Cool completely and store at room temperature.

Glazed Apple Hand Pies
Dawn Vaughn

Lucia comes over every other Friday and we always cook together. One day we decided to make this recipe. At first she wanted to save her pie to eat once she was home, but when she finally tried one, she ate two of them before leaving our house. She took several pies home to share with her family.

Ingredients

1 box (14.1 oz) refrigerated pie crust (for 2 pies)
¼ C unsalted butter
2 C diced and peeled Crunch Pak Apples (about 24-30 slices or 2 large apples)
¼ t Kosher salt
¼ t nutmeg
¼ C light brown sugar, packed
1 t cinnamon
2 T flour
1 egg white, beaten
Glaze –1 ¼ C powdered sugar and 2 T milk

Instructions

Remove pie crust from package and allow to come to room temperature. Preheat oven to 425 and prepare filling.

Dice and peel Crunch Pak Apple slices. In large skillet, melt butter over medium high heat. Add apples, salt, nutmeg, brown sugar, and cinnamon. Heat for about 5-10 minutes. Or until apples are soft, stirring occasionally.

While apples are heating, unroll pie crusts and cut 6-7 circles from each crust (using a 4" biscuit cutter.) You may have to roll scraps to get extra circles. Set aside.

After apples have softened, sprinkle in flour. Heat for additional minute, stirring thoroughly.

Using a 1 Tablespoon scoop, drop apple mixture into center of each pie circle. Fold in half and pinch edges completely. Poke hand pie with tines of fork to prevent bursting. Beat egg white in a small bowl. Brush over the tops of each pie. Bake on parchment paper lined baking sheet for 15-20 minutes or until lightly browned. While pies are baking, whisk together glaze ingredients. Remove cooked pies from baking sheet and drop on gaze, coating it completely. Return to parchment paper and allow to set for about 10 minutes. Enjoy warm or cold.

Easy Peasy Pudding Cookies
Virginia White

I think this recipe arrived at our house when our youngest daughter, Kari, received this in first grade. We made it several times while she was young and I brought it out when I started cooking with the grandkids. It has been a huge hit!

Ingredients
3 C biscuit mix
2 boxes (any flavor) instant pudding (reg. size)
1 C oil
2 eggs

Instructions
Preheat oven to 375. Mix all ingredients together. Roll into balls and then place on cookie sheet about 2" apart. Flatten with a fork. Bake 13-15 minutes.

You can roll dough balls in sugar if desired before you bake them. Let set for 2-3 minutes before removing from the pan onto a cooling rack or cutting board.

If you decide to use chocolate pudding, you can add chocolate chips.

Any Time Scrambled Eggs
Kaycee Dulany

My big sister, Sheridan, and my big brother, Garrett, used to make scrambled eggs and I always liked them and wanted to know how to make them myself. Sometimes I like to make them just for myself and sometimes I make them for the family. When Mom comes home from work, she is sometimes very tired, so I decide to make dinner. It is always scrambled eggs because I love to make them and they are good for you. Sometimes I fix bacon and toast with them.

Ingredients

3 eggs if you make them for one person. 10 eggs if you make them for the family
Milk—I eyeball the amount of milk to put in the bowl with the eggs
Butter to melt in the skillet
American cheese to taste – broken into pieces
Salt and pepper to taste

Instructions

After you get all the eggs cracked and in a bowl, add the milk. Beat with a fork.
Put a little butter in the skillet to melt before you pour the egg mixture in.
Break up a few slices of American cheese and put on top of the egg mixture.
Stir the egg and cheese mixture for 3-5 minutes.
When they are done just the way you like them, dish them up and use salt and pepper to taste. I love pepper.

Witches Brew Snack
Virginia White

When my daughters were small, they wanted to have a Halloween party. We decorated the house, especially the basement with "scary" decorations, and had a number of activities. We blindfolded the kids and provided a bowl with sliced grapes (eyeballs), cooked spaghetti (intestines) my husband found a mannequin leg (don't ask) on one of his walks, so we had it sticking out of a top shelf in a storage closet with "blood" (red paint) on it, and bobbed for apples. But we had to have snacks too. I made some Halloween decorated cupcakes, but also had graham crackers decorated. I don't think mine were quite like this, but when I found this in our church cookbook, I was reminded of our first Halloween party.

Ingredients
Ghost Dust – 2 C powdered sugar
Moon Drop – milk
Earth – ¼ C cocoa
Owl's Blood - 2-3 T maraschino cherry juice
Frog's eyes – chocolate bits
Broom straw – coconut
Grasshopper spit – 1 t vanilla
Fence Post – graham crackers

Instructions
Add sugar, cocoa, juice, vanilla, and enough milk to make a spread like frosting. Spread it on graham crackers. Decorate with chocolate bits and coconut.

Salt Dough
Staci Day

This recipe is much like Play-Doh, but can be baked to a permanent finish. This is a great non-toxic option for dough that you can play with and that you can bake and keep your creations. A very cool thing to do.

Ingredients
2 cups all-purpose flour plus some for kneading the dough
1 cup salt
¾-1 cup cold water

Instructions
Mix flour and salt together in a bowl. Slowly mix water, a few tablespoons at a time, into flour mixture until dough is smooth and easy to handle. Knead dough for 10 minutes and let rest for 20 minutes.

Preheat oven to 250 degrees F. (120 degrees C)

Form dough into desired shapes and arrange on a baking sheet.

Bake in a preheated oven until dry and hard, about 2 hours. Allow to cool completely.

Note From Virginia White: Kaycee and I made this and she used cookie cutters for some of her decorations and did a little freelance on other decorations. She had fun painting them after they dried.

Also, you will need so have a little flour on the board for kneading.

Paper Clay
Staci Day

This is a fantastic way of recycling paper to turn into anything you can imagine. It is a wonderful building material that doesn't require heat to set it before it can be painted and because it is paper, it is light and can be used to make a variety of objects without a lot of weight. It takes the old Paper Mache up to the next level.

Ingredients
shredded paper or newspaper cut into pieces
large bowl
hot water
flour – 1 part flour to 4 parts paper pulp
salt
a hand blender or mixer
Optional: white glue

Instructions
Begin by shredding all your paper. Using shredded paper is a wonderful recycling technique.

Fill a bowl with paper and hot water. Hot water will help to break the fibers of the paper down quicker. You want the paper to turn into mush so the hot water helps this process along. Leave overnight (or for a few hours). Your mixture won't look much different the next day, but the paper should now be softer and ready for hand blending!

Blend with a hand blender or similar. This step helps to get all of the paper fibers broken own to their smallest point and ready for mixing. The smaller fibers also makes the clay smoother.

Squeeze out excess water, but save some to add back in if needed to make your clay the right consistency.

Add flour and salt to your paper pulp mixture. The flour will help to give the paper clay some structure. The amount of flour will vary depending on the consistency of clay you want. Add enough to give some body, but not so much as to dry the paper pulp out so that it falls apart. The salt will help to prevent mold from growing in the clay.

At this stage you can add some glue to the mix if you want. Glue will make the clay extra sticky and will give it a different consistency. This stage is all about how the paper clay feels so get your hands in there and get messy!

Storing your paper clay – use an air tight container. This will store in an air tight container in the fridge for 2-3 weeks.

Note: Because the base of this is flour and not glue, there is a unique smell to this DIY paper clay. But it is an organic, natural smell. Once you have painted your work and once it is fully dry, it will pass. You CAN use glue as mentioned.

Made in the USA
Columbia, SC
18 November 2021

49112790R00122